Praise for *A Cancer Odyssey*

"In this engrossing book of vulnerabilities and social support, David Snow, a prominent sociologist, bravely shares his cancer experience, combined with the disruption of contracting a serious case of COVID and the less commonly seen description of being in a clinical trial with major side-effects. Insights from medical writers and sociologists are wisely interspersed but never break up the narrative. Anyone suffering from cancer can learn about the inner, social, family, and biomedical lives of the sick person. Social scientists can learn the experience of illness through creative autoethnography. Physicians and nurses can learn about the travails of navigating a complexity of different treatments and the kind of support their patients need."

—**PHIL BROWN, PhD,** distinguished professor of sociology and director, Social Science Environmental Health Research Institute, Northeastern University

"A captivating read about the odyssey of a cancer survivor who writes in liminal prose about the boundary between wellness and cancer and the changes that come with that transition. He compellingly describes this journey of dealing with cancer, fighting COVID during the treatment, and the successes and complications of participating in a clinical trial. I found it thoughtful and eminently readable."

—**SUSAN O'BRIEN, MD,** hematologist/oncologist; professor, UC Irvine School of Medicine

"As a physician and cancer survivor, I thought the feelings and challenges presented in *A Cancer Odyssey* would be old hat for me. Instead, I was so impressed and amazed by Dr. Snow's masterful evaluation and dissection of those feelings and issues, and by his profound insights. He is a skilled raconteur as well! I wish I had this book as I went through my own cancer odyssey!"

—*JEVELYN YONCHAR, MD,* diplomate,
American Board of Internal Medicine

"Professor Snow's up-close account of his cancer odyssey during the COVID-19 era brings to bear his career's worth of experience as a social scientist, offering keen sociological insight into his and his loved ones' grappling with cancer—the 'emperor of all maladies.' This book peels back the curtain on the realities of navigating serious illness, illuminating experiences that are both deeply personal and profoundly shaped by broader social forces. Snow has something to teach all of us about such a journey, whether you are a clinician, researcher, patient, or supporting a loved one through their own healthcare odyssey."

—*DANIEL SMITHERS, MD, MS,* attending internist,
Brigham & Women's Hospital; research fellow, Harvard Medical School

A Cancer ODYSSEY

Navigating Cancer, COVID, and a Clinical Trial During the Pandemic Years

DAVID A. SNOW

This book is an autoethnographic memoir reflecting the author's recollections of his odyssey-like medical journey over time. Its story and its words, except where quoted or referenced, are the author's, but the narrative is woven together with and through the involvement of others who have accompanied the author on his journey, none of whom are mentioned by name to ensure their anonymity, other than his present and late wives.

Published by River Grove Books
Austin, TX
www.rivergrovebooks.com

Distributed by River Grove Books, an imprint of Greenleaf Book Group

Design and composition by Greenleaf Book Group and Jonathan Lewis
Cover design by Greenleaf Book Group and Jonathan Lewis
Cover image used under license from ©Adobestock.com/Success
Media Paper texture from Kiwihug on Unsplash.

Publisher's Cataloging-in-Publication data is available.

Print ISBN: 979-8-90052-031-5

eBook ISBN: 979-8-90052-032-2

First Edition

For Roberta, my wife, best friend,
and odyssey companion, and my three children—
Heather, Maggie, and Pete—who have
endured cancer for too much of their lives,
especially through their late mother's long battle,
and then through mine.

Contents

Preface

An odyssey is a kind of journey, but a very particular one. Unlike most journeys that have an anticipated destination or outcome, an odyssey has a desired destination, but it is often an improbable one because of the obstacles repeatedly encountered along the way. The legendary essence of the term, its historic lodestone, is Homer's original epic poem, *The Odyssey*, wherein the mythical Greek hero Odysseus spends ten years in an ambiguous, obstacle-ridden expedition in his attempt to return home to Ithaca after fighting in the Trojan War. Over two thousand years later, after the first written accounts of Odysseus's mythic journey, sociologist Neil Smelser's sweeping analysis of the odyssey experience describes it as a journey marked by the disruption and destructuring of everyday routines and life, a state of liminality or fluctuating ambiguity between life as it was and as currently experienced, and the threat of various obstacles and dangers encumbering the journey en route to some targeted goal of recovery, rebirth, renewal or return, supposedly marking the end of the odyssey experience.[1]

In many respects, being diagnosed with and treated for cancer is that kind of journey. It is an odyssey laden with challenges and uncertainties, which are compounded in the course of treatment regimens and, for some, clinical trials. Of course, there is also an idealized destination or goal: It's being cured.

But there is little consensual agreement in oncology as to what "cured" means, with both oncologists and patients often hesitant to use the word.[2] A more measurable and resonant goal is complete remission, which is achieved when there isn't any evidence of cancer on the basis of blood work, imaging tests, and physical exams. Learning that one has attained complete remission is a source of great relief, of course, but it doesn't mean cured. It means that there is no detectable evidence of what is called minimal or measurable residual disease (MRD). Consequently, hearing that one is in complete remission carries two messages: one is that you have been issued a welcome reprieve, the other is that you are not out of the woods. Rather, you are in a liminal state of active observation, often depressingly called "watch and wait" or "watch and worry." So, unlike Odysseus's experience, marked finally by his return home and eventual embrace of his wife Penelope and son Telemachus, the cancer odyssey continues without such a clear cut ending in sight. There is a desired outcome, for sure, but it is an indeterminate one.

Introduction

Illness is the night-side of life, a more onerous citizenship. Everyone who is born holds dual citizenship, in the kingdom of the well and the kingdom of the sick. Although we all prefer to use only the good passport, sooner or later each of us is obliged, at least for a spell, to identify ourselves as citizens of the other space.

—SUSAN SONTAG[1]

My odyssey-like journey into the realm of cancer within the kingdom of the sick began in the fall of 2017. My now eight-year odyssey wasn't just encumbered by cancer of various kinds. I also experienced and tested positive for COVID for forty-five days and had to navigate its ongoing threat because of being immunocompromised. Even more troublesome were several noxious medication-induced side effects of the fifteen-month clinical trial I joined in midsummer of 2021—side effects that aren't curable and will travel with me for the rest of my life.

This is my story of that odyssey, of living with and navigating three different intersecting cancers, COVID, and a clinical trial and its adverse side effects during the pandemic years.

This book falls into the literary genre of memoirs. But not so tightly or neatly. Odysseys may be a variant of memoirs, but they are not a defining feature. Memoirs are generally thought of as personal stories about one's life or a bracketed segment of one's life, typically narrated chronologically as a journey from one point in time to another. This book encompasses this defining characteristic, but it also differs in two important respects: First, as an odyssey, it is a distinctive kind of journey fraught with obstacles of danger and disruptive ambiguity.

The book's second distinctive feature is even more important: It is an autoethnography rather than just a personally narrated accounting of my journey. An autoethnography is a variant of an ethnography, a long-standing research method within anthropology and sociology. An ethnography entails the study of people and their associations within their natural contexts with an emphasis on grasping how things are experienced and understood from the vantage point of those studied. Simply put, an ethnography seeks to provide a compelling, resonant understanding of what it's like to live and walk in the shoes of those studied. An autoethnography does much the same, but with a focus on the author-researcher's lived experiences, rather than on others'. It is thus a blend of ethnography and autobiography with respect to a segment of one's life and how they have experienced it, but with methodological kinship with the field notes and journaling of ethnography and an analytic thrust of drawing on relevant theoretical insights to generate resonant links to broader social, cultural, political, and historical contexts.[2]

When I first began my cancer odyssey, my journaling or note-taking was sporadic. Occasionally I would log my experience and fluctuating feelings, but I was reluctant to do so consistently. I was concerned it would focus too much of my attention on my condition. I was no stranger to how journaling could become somewhat of an obsessive daily ritual. For the better part of a year after my first wife, Judy, passed away in 2005,

I maintained a detailed grieving log on an almost daily basis. It clearly helped quell my understandable grief,[3] but looking back I came to think that it focused too much attention on my loss, thus functioning as an unintended roadblock to moving forward. I didn't want that to happen again, as I was still employed full-time and engaged in my teaching and research obligations at the time of my cancer diagnosis. But as my cancer progressed at the outset of the pandemic and I joined a clinical trial, the note-taking and journaling became regularized features of my odyssey.

As with any autobiographic or autoethnographic memoir, this story is not only mine. It is a narrative that is woven together with and through the involvement of others who have accompanied me on the journey. These fellow travelers include Roberta, my partner of twenty years and wife for ten, who was by my side for every appointment, asking questions and taking notes just as I was, and unfailingly providing reassuring comfort. Other fellow travelers include my three adult children, grandchildren, my siblings and their families, friends and acquaintances, my oncology team and other physicians who joined the odyssey as new and unanticipated medical issues arose, and even deceased relatives, particularly Judy, my first wife of thirty-seven years and mother of our three children, whose encounters with breast cancer and its metastasis were baked into me and colored my experiences with and thoughts about the cancer experience. All are contributors to the story, obviously in various ways with different effects. It is my telling, of course, but the story I tell would be a different one without those who traveled with me in one way or another. And this is especially true of Roberta, for whom this odyssey, and thus this book, is as much hers as mine.

My telling would also be different if it weren't for my sociological sensitivity to the broader social contexts in which our personal lives and challenges are embedded. During the course of the odyssey I was reminded repeatedly that "neither the life of an individual nor the history of a society can be understood without understanding both," as C. Wright Mills wrote in his mid-twentieth century, but still relevant, treatise titled *The Sociological Imagination.*[4] Its essence, he argued, resides in awareness of the relationship between events in one's personal life and events in one's social milieu and society, between what he dubbed "personal troubles" and "social or public issues." Cancer, whatever its variant or stage, is unquestionably a personal trouble or challenge. And how it's experienced and dealt with is partly contingent on social processes and structures in the enveloping world. It is because of this sociological truism that I situate my cancer experience within the COVID pandemic years of 2020–2024. As the telling of my journey unfolds, the social environment that impacted its character should become evident, as hopefully will the more general link between personal troubles and public issues.

But why my story? What about my journey might be of interest to others, especially in light of the millions of those in the US alone who have been afflicted with some form of cancer and perhaps even saddled with COVID as well?[5] Don't they all have their own stories? Indeed, they do. But they are rarely told in a wider circle than among one's intimates, and the telling is usually oral. Moreover, while each has their own story, those stories are not uniformly unique. As suggested by the Susan Sontag quote at the outset, there are commonalities among those who have slipped into some state of illness by virtue of incumbency in a role for which one didn't sign up, is ill prepared, and is laden with ambiguity about what's involved, the length of the incumbency, and when and where the illness journey might end.

In his book *The Lonely Patient: How We Experience Illness*, Dr. Michael Stein similarly portrays the experience of illness as "a kind of travel" into a foreign landscape wherein "the sick person wonders with mounting anxiety: What am I supposed to do? What am I supposed to think? How long will I be forced to stay? Who can I talk to? Why am I here? Where do I go next?"[6] I can vouch for the salience of these questions based on their resonance with my experiences and those of family and friends who have asked these and other such questions in their journeys that preceded mine into this landscape of illness. For these reasons, I believe that my odyssey is not personally unique but resonates in ways with the journey of most people living with cancer. There is something about cancer that is shared by all who have or are currently experiencing it, independent of its type or stage. It has a way of taking up residence in one's being, not just physiologically but psychologically and sociologically as well.

My aim is to explore and extend our understanding of the reach of what is perhaps the most frightening and vexing illness that oncologist Siddhartha Mukherjee has called "the emperor of all maladies."[7] I want to illuminate how cancer touches and intersects with every aspect of one's life, from relations with intimates and extended family to friends, colleagues, and even acquaintances. Indeed, I found cancer intruding on the character and organization of my everyday activities, including my consciousness and identity, my professional work, my exercise routine and sexual relations, and even my dreams. My experience is that whether or not one's cancer is physiologically metastatic, its reach into the corners of one's life has a radical metastatic character to it. It leaves little, if anything, about one's life untouched, including one's consciousness, as it has a way of insidiously inscribing itself therein as a haunting reminder, even when in remission, of what you once experienced and could again.

By telling the story of my journey, indeed my odyssey, I hope it will help those who are or will be traveling down this same path—either as patients or caregivers, as well as physicians and medical staff—understand from a patient's standpoint the metastatic reach of cancer beyond the body and the experience of negotiating its effects and the complications that may arise with its treatment.

Like Odysseus's journey, mine has been an uncertain one, laden with obstacles and challenges, but always with the hope of navigating through or around them, and with the goal of recovery and return to a semblance of life before the odyssey began.

Blood in the Urine

It was a beautiful, sunny Southern California Sunday afternoon in early October. I had just returned home from a mile lap swim, and had been scanning through the Sunday *New York Times* while watching the LA Rams game when I went to the nearest bathroom to urinate. I looked down at the toilet bowl and, to my shock, saw a bloody-colored bowl of liquid. And it persisted whenever I needed to pee throughout the remainder of the day and into Monday.

Even though I wasn't experiencing associated pain, my wife Roberta and I feared the gross blood in the urine signaled that something serious was awry. So on early Monday afternoon with heightened alarm, we went to the nearby university walk-in clinic. I took with me a jar of the blood-infused urine so the attending medical staff could see it as well. They sent us to the university hospital emergency room. Because I wasn't complaining about chest pains and didn't have difficulty breathing or indication of severe injury, the emergency room attendant told us to grab a couple of seats and wait. After doing so for what seemed like well over an hour, I asked one of the attendants when I might be seen. He said since I was not experiencing any cardiovascular problems or visibly bleeding, "It could still be a while."

It was then that I showed him the jar of bloody liquid, which caught his attention. Within about fifteen minutes, I was called in to see the ER physician, who took my vitals, including my weight. After I explained what was going on, he speculated that the blood may be due to a kidney stone, but I was doubtful. I wasn't experiencing the clenching pain often triggered by passing kidney stones. In any case, the physician ordered a CT scan and then sent us back to the waiting room.

As we awaited the results, I commented to Roberta that I weighed seven pounds less than my normal weight, which caught me by surprise. She reminded me, however, that my appetite appeared to have declined recently. These two observations gave me pause, prompting me to think again that maybe something serious was at work. Trying to stymie the thought, I turned to my cell phone, checked my email, and tapped on ESPN.

After another hour or so passed, we were called into a private exam room. The ER physician blurted out, without any prefatory salutary comments, "You have two cancers: bladder cancer and lymphoma." The scan had revealed a tumor on the bladder and enlarged lymph nodes. Roberta and I were both shocked, physically and emotionally. Roberta remembers hearing his words as she stared at the wood-paneled wall, an unforgettable scene, like knowing what you were looking at when you learned the Twin Towers had come down. We looked at each other with tears welling in our eyes and searching for words to capture what we had just heard. But none were forthcoming, as we were both speechless.

The physician admitted me to the hospital. "While you could go home and come back in the morning," he said, "it's probably better to be admitted now. That way, further tests and plans for the surgical extraction of the tumor and the lymph node can proceed as soon as possible." He added that there was the possibility of small blood clots forming in the urethra, which could impede urination and be painful to pass. "If that happens," he stressed, "we could deal with it here right away."

After getting settled in a small, narrow room tucked at the end of a short corridor in the original wing of the hospital, I told Roberta she should go home rather than spend a restless and sleepless night on a rollaway bed. Neither of us had come prepared, and we had a five-month old pup at home that needed to be let out and monitored. But she didn't leave right away; we talked with my three adult children, although haltingly because our conversations were interspersed with tears and the search for the right words, due I suspect to our culturally limited vocabulary for moments like this. It's just hard to know what to say.

She drove home alone around 10:30 p.m. So there I lay, stretched out on a hospital bed with my left arm hooked up to an IV line and a catheter running from my bladder into a urine bag hanging on the side of the bed that measured the volume of urine and monitored the amount of bleeding. Although I didn't feel much in the way of physical discomfort other than the agitation of the IV line and the catheter, I did feel palpable anxiety and a sense of dread that perhaps this was the beginning of a downward slide. It wasn't depression as clinically understood—an immobilizing mood disorder that entails persistent feelings of sadness and disinterest in perusing normal everyday activities and encounters.[1] I may have been close to that kind of depression, but I fought it off. It was more like feeling the "blues"; I was gloomy and disheartened.

But it wasn't the gloom and associated despair that gripped my mind. It was fear. Not only fear of what tomorrow or the next several days would reveal about the severity of my two cancers, but just generalized fear of this "emperor of all maladies." There are few feelings or emotions that can occupy consciousness and focus its attention like fear, principally because it connotes a threat and vulnerability. Because of this, some neuroscientists have argued metaphorically that "fear resembles a dictator that makes all other brain processes (from cognition to breathing) its slave." It has "authoritarian command over the rest of the brain."[2]

Among the illnesses generative of such fear, few are as galvanizing and lingering as cancer because of its duality as both a potentially embodied and broadly out-of-the-body metastatic condition. Regarding the fear it spawns, surveys of adults across a number of countries, including the United States, have found it to be the most dreaded disease.[3] This fear is due in large measure, according to a review of research on the stigma and fear of cancer, to "the perceived severity of the illness, its association with severe suffering and physical limitations, and the belief that cancer is a death sentence."[4] Even though I knew that the duration of survival varies by the type of cancer and its staging, and that advances in treatment alternatives have extended the survival rate for many cancers and tempered long-standing stigmatizing stereotypes, these stereotypic fears would haunt me throughout the odyssey.[5] Understandably, I started to psychologically circle the wagons. After all, being told you have two cancers—one in an organ and the other in the blood and lymphatic system, suggesting that metastasis may already have occurred—seemed strikingly foreboding, even though there were no details at the moment on the cancers' severity. The diagnostic details would have to await the surgical extraction of the tumor and a lymph node and the eventual lab results.

Once Roberta returned home, we spoke a number of times, reassuring each other the best we could, and I made plans to call my four siblings back east in the morning. Other than that, I couldn't really think about who else should be included in the circle. My guess, based on the passing of my late wife, Judy, as well as that of her younger sister, our parents, and others, is that the final circle would be quite small. *Maybe I'll think more broadly when tomorrow comes*, I thought. *Or maybe I'll realize that it is way too premature to even think about circling the wagons.* Not the kinds of thoughts conducive to drifting off to sleep, which I eventually did for a few hours with the help of several melatonin. Thinking about it further was too overwhelming.

The melatonin-induced sleep provided a modicum of escape until six o'clock in the morning when I was jarringly awakened by the bright overhead lights being flicked on, a knock on the door swinging open, and someone saying, "Good morning, Mr. Snow. This is the oncology team making morning rounds." The attending physician came in, followed by a fellow, an intern, and some medical students, a tight squeeze for four to six people to crowd in next to the computer stand, with one or two needing to stand out in the hall holding the door open. They crowded in to get a look at me and ask a few questions about how I was doing and feeling. Although I felt pretty normal physically, aside from the IV line and the catheter, I didn't offer much in the way of specifics since I didn't have any sense of what or how I should feel other than being alarmed that I'd just discovered that I had two different cancers and was hospitalized awaiting surgery.

I did have a few questions, though. I was particularly interested in learning more about my cancers. "Is it unusual to be diagnosed with two different cancers at the same time?" I asked. "Are the two cancers independent or connected via metastasis? Whether independent or connected, which one likely came first? What is likely to have caused them? And is one more concerning than the other?" They acknowledged the questions, but they weren't willing to offer much in the absence of lab diagnostics on the yet-to-be-scheduled surgical excision of the bladder tumor and one of my lymph nodes. That surgery was still a few days away and the lab diagnostics further out.

Given their reticence to say much about my situation other than that it was serious, I became the inquisitor, querying them about their education and decision to specialize in oncology. "Where did you go to medical school? What about undergraduate school? How and why did you end up here? Why oncology?" Although I had plenty of time to kill, that's not really what I was trying to do. In learning about their medical educational journeys, I hoped to hear that they had all gone to reputable schools to reassure myself I would be in the hands of a team of superbly trained and highly competent specialists. But what I really wanted was to allay my mounting anxieties about the forthcoming surgery, the eventual pathology diagnostics, and the journey I began last night in the emergency room without any sense of where it would take me and how it might end.

After the oncology entourage came the urology team, followed by cardiologists (because of a low pulse rate or bradycardia), a surgical squad, and a few anesthesiologists. Given the extraordinary, specialized nature of modern medicine and my double-headed cancer, I wasn't surprised by the number of teams including me in their morning rounds. I was curious, though, whether these specialty teams communicated with each other about their observations regarding my case. Was there someone who functioned as an information hub, pulling together relevant observations and coordinating procedural plans? This hospital ritual of morning rounds, which is most elaborated in university training hospitals with a lead physician and a trailing team, its members in order of years of instruction, repeated itself throughout the next several hours and days.

After a couple mornings of these rounds, I came to realize experientially what I had already sensed: interest in my status may not have been as important to the intern and student team members as the opportunity it provided for their firsthand exposure to real-life illnesses, their etiology, and possible treatment repertoires. I suspect this assessment of morning rounds doesn't hold for all such rounds since oftentimes the lead physician and her team are checking on the status of their patients. But the hospital hadn't yet assigned a specialist to track me, presumably because

I was awaiting surgery and a more detailed diagnostic report. Thus, the rounds, at least initially and as I experienced them, were first and foremost an instructional opportunity and occasion. My suspicion was reaffirmed several times when a team would huddle outside my room, still close enough to the door for me to overhear discussion of my case but without my being able to discern the particulars.

My curiosity triggered recall of the concept of "awareness contexts," which describes variation in the scope of knowledge about the patient's condition among the key participants. Two medical sociologists in the mid-1960s coined this term based on their research on dying in a hospital and the identification of different types of awareness contexts that capture the types of case-specific information that is shared between hospital staff—physicians, nurses, students, attendants—and the patient and her family.[6] On the other hand, the now widespread adoption of electronic health record (EHR) systems, which provide an electronic version of a patient's medical history and which is readily accessible to patients via access portals like MyChart, makes insulated awareness contexts more likely to disappear. But the degree to which patients are interested in the details of their condition can be quite variable. For Roberta and me, however, we were very much interested in knowing the specifics.

In short, I found myself thinking that the morning rounds were a context in which attention was focused on information gathering and sharing by the medical team, which was reserved for their own sequestered conversations. Whatever the case, clearly I felt like I was a subject of inquiry, a kind of metaphoric microbe under the microscope.

That doesn't mean that these rounds aren't useful from the patient's standpoint. To the contrary, they can be very beneficial, or at least that's how I found them. For one thing, they were comforting in that they let me know I wasn't being ignored and that my condition warranted instructional observation and discussion. I also found it reassuring to have more than one set of specialty-focused eyes on me, as did Roberta, who moved into my claustrophobic hospital room with me on day two. The daily rounds also provided a sounding board for a curious, inquisitive patient, as well as others, to talk with. Hospitals are busy places, with lots of interruptions aside from the morning rounds, but they can also be lonely places for the patients as they find themselves in an unfamiliar social world with few, if any, familiar faces. So I looked forward to the morning rounds.

It also became clear that some of the rounds-based observations were passed on to the hospitalist, thus addressing my initial curiosity. My hospitalist—a doctor charged with the personal coordination of my care—introduced himself on Tuesday afternoon of my first full day in the hospital. He, too, asked me how I was doing, how I felt, but he also tried to learn more about me, asking questions about my family, what I did, and where I lived. And I returned the compliment in kind, asking him this and that about himself. Among other things, I learned we grew up in the same Midwest state, that we both attended The Ohio State University at one time or another, and that he received his medical degree from Harvard. Our shared biographic information, along with his easy conversational style and seemingly genuine friendly manner, made me feel that he had my best interests in hand. And so he did, with his coordination and scheduling of my two surgeries back-to-back, thereby ensuring only one encounter with the anesthesiologist.

Even still, Roberta and I felt like we were floating in unknown waters, helping each other as best we could and searching for a lifeline around us, both querying the doctors and reaching out to people close to us who might provide a reassuring hand. We also sought additional medical information by contacting two long-term friends, a husband and wife who are both physicians. They immediately provided empathetic understanding and suggested we speak with their son, a practicing urologist. Shortly thereafter we had a conference call, where he provided more information about the diagnostic path ahead. He reassured us that we could contact him at any time. Although we didn't call because we didn't want to bother him, he called us again, which was reassuring, in spite of the lack of definitive information.

After four days of uncertainty and three days after being admitted, the surgeries took place on Thursday afternoon of October 12. During the preparation for the bladder surgery, the urologist asked if I had smoked for any length of time; he noted that smoking increases the risk of bladder cancer by causing harmful chemicals to be excreted into the urine, which can damage the lining of the bladder.

"Unfortunately," I said, "I smoked about a pack a day of Marlboro Lights for around fourteen years, but quit over forty years ago."

"Well, it's great that you quit," he said, "but that you smoked as you did, coupled with your age and being male, might be a reason you have bladder cancer."

I had no basis for disagreeing, but I was still curious if whatever variant of lymphoma I have might be the primary cancer, with the bladder cancer following as the secondary one. What I knew, or at least thought I did on the basis of my discussions with the hospitalist, is that lymphoma can make one vulnerable to some other cancers.

The two surgeons—the general surgeon for the lymph node and the oncology urologist for the tumor excision—assured me that the surgeries would go fine, but I was less concerned about the surgeries than what they might reveal. Lying on the gurney in the cold operating suite, hearing the staff as they made their preparations, I anxiously awaited the anesthesiologist to put me under so I wouldn't succumb to the pull of dark and bleak thoughts of devastating news that I actually was at the cusp of a downward slide.

CHAPTER 2

The Canary in the Mine and a New Diagnosis

The phrase "canary in the coal mine" denotes a person or thing that serves as an early warning sign for a coming crisis.

—CHRISTAL POLLOCK, DVM, DIPL ABVP[1]

Despite my apprehensions, both surgeries went well without any complications. First was surgical removal of a lymph node from under my left arm, followed by excision of the bladder tumor. Roberta was the first to know, when the urologist came out to explain the procedure and his findings, and she sent texts to our three children, the first of a great many communications she would be sending out over the years of treatment.

In the postop recovery room, the hospitalist and the general surgeon told me the reason for extracting a full-blown lymph node rather than just a splice was that the architecture of the lymph node provides a better read on the type of lymphoma. The urologist told me that the bladder tumor was a classic, transitional cell bladder cancer and that he was able to excise it with what appeared to be clear and clean margins. He also noted that it was caught early on, meaning that it had not spread beyond the inner layer of the bladder wall, which the postop pathology report's diagnosis confirmed as a "non-invasive low-grade urothelial carcinoma." So my prognosis was good. He noted, however, that bladder cancer is notorious for reoccurring, so I would have to schedule a cystoscopy every three months. That registered as a small price to pay for knowing that my bladder was now cancer-free, at least for the time being, and brought some closure to the four days Roberta and I had spent in the hospital.

Clearly, the urologic oncologist's postsurgical assessment of the bladder cancer provided a measure of reassurance regarding its diagnostic and prognostic status, and I felt lucky. Two of my friends had had advanced-stage bladder cancer by the time it was discovered, with one dying in a few years and the other requiring bladder excision and reconstruction with a portion of the intestine. He later endured metastasis for a number of years prior to his passing. Familiarity with their cases made me wonder what accounted for my luck of discovering the cancer in its early stages. The answer was the blood in the urine that sent me to the emergency room. It was the canary in the coal mine, not only for the bladder cancer but for the lymphoma as well. One of the ironies of illness and medicine is that what initially may trigger trepidation may turn out to be a blessing in disguise. Had my two friends had such an early warning sign, they might still be here today.

This was one of many instances where I felt relief, even in the face of unpleasant news and experiences. Considered psychologically, relief is a feeling of pleasant surprise or reassurance, of happiness, that something unpleasant and worrisome has not transpired or has ended, triggering a concurrent release from stress and anxiety. Embedded in this definition are two types of relief: "counterfactual" relief, triggered by avoidance of something unwelcome, such as surgery; and "temporal" relief, sparked by the cessation of a trying challenge or situation, as with completion of a treatment regimen.[2]

My experience with the counterfactual form of relief was probably most memorable during the first couple weeks of the journey. There was the initial anxious wait in the emergency room wondering what was going on, followed by hospitalization and the wait for a more concrete diagnosis, trailed by almost two weeks of waiting for an overall assessment and assignment to an oncologist specializing in my variant of lymphoma. No tangible relief was forthcoming when the emergency room physician told me that I had two cancers, other than perhaps the slight sigh of relief elicited by the preliminary diagnosis and naming of what was a worrisome known unknown—the gross blood in the urine—thus transforming it into a known known. But I did feel considerable relief when the postsurgical diagnoses revealed that the bladder cancer and lymphoma were in the early stages and not as immediately critical as I had feared.

Similarly, I was reassured two weeks later when the oncology urologist confirmed the postsurgical assessment and connected me with an oncologist specializing in my variant of lymphoma. Both instances muted my most dire diagnostic fears and relieved my anxieties. As is often the case when unknowns are identified and named, the new known may still not be desirable or what one hoped for, but it is likely to provide some sense of relief since it reduces the anxiety of not knowing what is going on and what one is confronting. Clearly, I wasn't happy about the dual cancer diagnosis, albeit in the early stages, but knowing what I was dealing with was much less unnerving than being in the dark.

But the character of the lymphoma was still broadly open-ended. Given that there are more than seventy types of lymphoma, with considerable variation in their seriousness, treatment, and prognosis, I anxiously awaited the pathology report on the excised lymph node from under my left arm. *What kind of lymphoma is it?* I wondered. *Is it Hodgkin or non-Hodgkin lymphoma? Is it aggressive or slow growing? What are the treatment alternatives and their prognostic prospects?* I learned that the answers to these and other questions that would arise were neither immediately nor predictably forthcoming. Rather, these questions surfaced sporadically over time, in a piecemeal fashion contingent on what symptoms I was reporting, the clinical and lab exam results, and the effects of the prescribed treatment, if any. The summary lab assessment of the excised lymph node was issued in the afternoon of the day after surgery, almost twenty-four hours later, and captured in the hospitalist's signed report that the on-duty RN handed to me prior to my release.

The hospitalist told me that I had chronic lymphocytic leukemia (CLL), which is a type of non-Hodgkin B cell lymphoma. The summary interpretation of the report was even more specific, noting clearly that what I had was small lymphocytic lymphoma (SLL). The report read:

> There is a diffuse proliferation of small mature lymphocytes which are mainly B cells. The B cells are positive for BCL2, CD5, CD20, CD 23 and PAX 5, consistent with small lymphocytic lymphoma. The proliferation rate is up to 15–20%. The immunophenotype is consistent with small lymphocytic lymphoma.

Even though I now had a more specific diagnosis for the initial, general diagnosis of lymphoma, I was still in the dark as to what it meant. Not being a physician, it would have helped me to have had a distillation of the medical jargon, but no one offered me one. Just the summary report. Roberta and I puzzled over the findings (as we would many times along the diagnostic and treatment path), often initially feeling at a loss, lacking information, asking ourselves how two educated people could be searching for a more definitive understanding. We knew that there are a lot of unknowns in medicine and health care, but still wondered how much others within the kingdom of the sick understood about their condition and treatment, and whether they, too, were grasping for information. Or, perhaps, they didn't want to know anything beyond what their doctors and other providers were saying and were doing.

I returned home with the report and a stash of new pills to staunch the pain of my spastic bladder along with a urinary catheter and the collection bag hanging from my belt into which it emptied. The catheter and bag, and the sporadic spasms, were aggravating, as they conspired to reduce my mobility and keep me housebound until removal of the catheter a week and a half later. But the anxiety that the vague diagnostic particulars and prognostic unknowns generated was more distressing.

During this time I became increasingly restless, not only because of my limited physical mobility, but also because I felt uncertain about what to tell people who might wonder about my whereabouts. Since I was still fully employed as a sociology professor at the University of California, Irvine, I needed to tell my department head I would likely be absent for a couple of weeks. I wondered, though, *How much could or should I say given my own uncertainties? And what about other colleagues with whom I was often in communication?* I ruminated about this for a few days, and then decided to send an email to the department head and a number of colleagues and professional friends, around a dozen in all.

Shortly after sending the email, I had second thoughts. I wondered about the burden I placed on colleagues by inviting a response to my medical challenge. It is not easy for many folks to find the right words other than to draw on the limited repertoire of Hallmark bromides. I was also concerned that by disclosing that I had been diagnosed with two cancers, but without any diagnostic details or prognostic prospects, I may have been suggesting that I was on the front end of a downward slide, making their responses even more cumbersome.

But most troubling of all was my concern about conveying the impression that I was taking up psychological residence in the disease itself. The last thing I wanted to do at the time was to make cancer the cloak I wore. I didn't want it to be my signifying identity. In his book on illness, as experienced principally by his patients, Michael Stein writes that by virtue of entering the kingdom of illness, one is "issued a new identity card."[3] This may be true, particularly if one's illness is visibly marked physically, as with bodily disfigurement or noticeable unintended weight loss, for example. But being issued an illness identity card doesn't mean that it must be routinely in play and granted greater salience than all of one's other identities.

Having a background in social psychology, I was well aware that how we see ourselves and project our identity is partly contingent on how others see us. More than a century ago, the famed American social psychologist Charles Horton Cooley coined the concept of the "looking glass self," suggesting that how one sees and feels about oneself—that is, their self-concept or sense of self—is largely dependent on how they imagine others perceive and evaluate them.[4] We all have multiple views of ourselves or identities contingent on the roles we assume or play, such as physician, professor, or parent, and the social categories to which we belong, such as gender, racial, ethnic, and national categories. Together, they constitute our social identities. But what determines which of these identities is most salient as we negotiate our daily routines and interact with others who populate those routines?[5] The congruence between our own view of self and our various identities matters. Do we see ourselves more in terms of one or two identities than other ones? The relevance of the identity to the situation or context also matters, but having a situationally imputed identity doesn't mean we have to claim and announce it.

A case in point. In my earlier research on homelessness with a former student and colleague, we found that even visibly homeless individuals often alternated between embracing and distancing themselves from that identity.[6] For instance, a fellow whose street name was "Gypsy Bill" would sometimes announce that he was "an expert dumpster diver," embracing that identity with pride, while at other times distancing himself from it and homelessness more generally. Like other homeless individuals we encountered, he said in so many words, "I can tell you about being homeless, but that's not who I am."

Based on subsequent research in other contexts, it became clear that the tension between identity embracement and distancing is quite common. Many years ago, in the week surrounding the wedding of one of my daughters, for example, Judy—who was still in the clutch of traditional chemotherapy for the metastasis of her breast cancer and who exuded the stereotypic symptoms—emphasized repeatedly to me and the immediate family, and to a half dozen close high school and college friends who came a few days ahead, that this was a celebration of her daughter's wedding, not a "pity party" for her. She didn't want people hovering over her and repeatedly asking how she was doing. Even though her appearance and prognosis called forth such questions, she did the best she could to reject that identity card. She wanted to accent the identities of the mother-of-the-bride and the wedding host, not that of a laboring cancer victim.

In the wake of such occurrences, the ill can expect a spate of questions: "Where have you been? What's been going on? How have you been doing? How are you now?" Not only did I often encounter these questions, but also it was often unclear how best to answer them. For one thing, I assumed that people don't usually ask such questions in hopes of soliciting detailed answers. Such questions, I thought, perhaps cynically, oiled the tracks for smooth interactional passage, much like saying "Nice to see you" or "Have a nice day" to the checkout cashier. But whether sincere or not, such questions don't mandate announcement of the cancer identity. Such concerns about the intersection of my cancer and my identity would continue to surface when friends and acquaintances, and even family, asked about my well-being, and especially so when the cancer progressed and I joined a long-term clinical trial.

This identity confusion aside, for now I was happy to be home, albeit anxiously awaiting removal of the catheter and the forthcoming postoperative meeting with my urologic oncologist surgeon to go over the final pathology report.

But I wouldn't receive diagnostic clarification of the initial report for another two weeks, so I impatiently forged ahead to get a better understanding by looking into published medical research. For one, I learned that the B cell positivity markers indicated in the report were tumor markers for CLL and SLL.[7] I figured that "diffuse proliferation" meant the SLL cancer cells had spread widely, given that cellular division is characteristic of most cells, with such division occurring as I write. I also knew that cellular division is a defining feature of cancer cells, but with a critical difference. Unlike most cells, the division characteristic of cancer cells is that it is unchecked, making them "capable of infinite rebirth." As oncologist Siddhartha Mukherjee explains in his chapter on cancer cells in *The Song of the Cell*, "Cancer is . . . a disorder of internal homeostasis: its hallmark is that cell division is dysregulated." Likening the regulators of such division to the accelerators and brakes in a car, Mukherjee writes:

> The genes that control these accelerators and brakes are broken—i.e., mutated—such that proteins that they encode, the

regulators of cell division, no longer function in their appropriate contexts. The accelerators are permanently jammed, or the brakes fail permanently. More typically, it is a combination of both events—jammed accelerator genes and snapped brakes—that drives the dysfunctional growth of a cancer cell.[8]

I suspected that the proliferation rate highlighted in the lab report referenced the rate at which my cancer cells were dividing. Even though there is no definitive cutoff for determining low and high proliferation rates, I learned that rates around 10 percent or less generally indicate slower division and less aggressive cancer, whereas rates in the neighborhood of 20 percent or higher suggest more rapid division.[9] My lab diagnostic rate of 15–20 percent meant that the proliferation rate for my affected B cells were intermediate but skewing high. This, coupled with the diffuse spread of the impacted cells, suggested that my variant of lymphoma was concerning. But I was still in a fog as to what I might make of it in comparison to other forms of cancer in terms of its seriousness, progression, and treatment. Even more particularly, I was curious about the similarity and difference between CLL and SLL.

Answers to these and other evolving questions would have to wait until the anticipated appointment on October 26 with my urologic oncologist and the CLL/SLL oncologist, to whom I would be referred. Roberta and I had been anxiously awaiting that appointment since leaving the hospital, so as the meeting approached, our apprehension increased.

I had a potent flashback recalling the psychologically tortuous times I experienced with Judy as we awaited the results of her latest exams and clinical assessments following her two bouts with breast cancer—the first in the spring of 1988 when she was forty-five and the last and terminal bout beginning in 2003. Sometimes the news was good, after which we would go for a celebratory lunch or dinner. Other times it was not only bad but devastating, particularly toward the end in early 2005 when my oldest sister and I took her to what was the last of her weekly appointments with her oncologist. Toward the end of the checkup, Judy asked, as she sat in her wheelchair, if she would ever walk again. The oncologist gently took her hands and held them, saying, "I think you have peaked, Judy. Just take each day at a time and enjoy it the best you can." My sister and I immediately were flushed with tears, as it was one of those moments in which the message was so painfully clear, not only in terms of what the oncologist said but also because of the surprisingly tender and gentle way in which he spoke. Given these past postexam assessments with Judy, it is hardly surprising that those experiences were called forth on this occasion and thus amplified my anxiety.

On the day of my appointment, not only did Roberta and I sit nervously in the medical center urology waiting room, but we both had to use the restroom several times, given that our joint anxiety had worked its way into our intestinal tracts. Right on cue.

Our anxiety dissipated as soon as the urologic oncologist, who had done the surgery, walked into the exam room with a reassuring smile that muffled the starkness of the barren, windowless room. He confidently reaffirmed his initial assessment of the bladder cancer, emphasizing that he had excised it with clean margins; he noted that the odds were pretty high that it would recur but could be treated. The key, he said, was continual monitoring via cystoscopies.

Turning to the CLL/SLL, he confirmed the lab report's diagnosis, but added that I had an indolent, chronic cancer, meaning nonaggressive, slow growing, and lingering. I initially found that puzzling—both diagnostically and prognostically—as I fearfully envisioned it as an aggressive cancer that would jump-start pretty much from its inception. I was relieved, yes, but perplexed.

My guess is that most people generally view cancer as an aggressive, hard-hitting affliction. That was my initial fear, which explains in part my thoughts about circling the wagons when I was first diagnosed. Considering that Judy's second round with breast cancer moved quickly and aggressively—its metastasis to the brain and liver was diagnosed only ten months prior to her passing—my perception was not surprising. Accenting my stereotypic conception even further was my sister-in-law's earlier passing only six months after being diagnosed with a soft tissue sarcoma.

Recalling Judy's cancer, as well as her sister's and that of other friends and relatives, their treatment regimens were initiated shortly on the heels of diagnosis. There was no cautionary monitoring, no watchful waiting. The protocol was to find the best current antidote, the standard-of-care treatment if there was one, and attack. It reminded me of when I used to garden and spotted a mound or two of foliage-eating ants. I didn't wait to observe the ants as they went about their genetically ritualized decimation of my freshly planted flora. Instead, I would disrupt the mounds and radiating pheromone trails with the current recommended antidote—usually a spray of vinegar and water. That's how I thought you would approach cancer, whatever the variety, upon its diagnosis.

Because of the nature of my SLL/CLL, my oncologist recommended that I not go into aggressive treatment right away but instead take a "watch and wait" approach. This put Roberta and me at ease for the moment, giving us some time to learn about it and how to monitor and treat it. For some types of nonaggressive cancers, like the SLL I had, neither early nor aggressive treatment is necessarily beneficial, and may even be counterproductive by triggering unwelcome side effects and reducing the possible effectiveness of down-the-road treatment due to increasing systemic resistance. Clearly my assumptions about cancer and cancer treatment were wrong. Watchful waiting didn't seem so misguided or confounding after all.[10]

My oncology urologist emphasized that "watch and wait" entailed actively monitoring the cancer rather than ignoring it. But for now, he stressed, it was especially important to see an oncologist specializing in this variant of lymphoma (something repeatedly emphasized a few years later in the CLL support group meetings I attended when I joined the clinical trial). Without hesitation, he assigned me to an in-house oncologist, who he said was one of the foremost experts on CLL/SLL in the country.

All of this was helpful, but we still didn't learn much new beyond the summary report I received prior to exiting the hospital. I soon realized, however, that the details and particulars weren't nearly as significant as the opportunity to meet face-to-face with a supportive physician who could humanize the lab reports. As sociologists with some research expertise in on-the-ground, face-to-face interaction, Roberta and I probably should have grasped more keenly the reassuring importance of discussing one's condition with the appropriate medical specialist. But our uncertainties and anxieties clearly overwhelmed us, even though we knew that the cancer was relatively dormant.

All we could do now was watch and wait.

CHAPTER 3

Watch and Wait and Diagnostic Indeterminacy

And "watch and wait" we did.

At the time, I was cautious about allowing my cancer diagnoses to become a preoccupation, as I was still employed full-time and engaged in my teaching and research obligations. No doubt, one might argue that such caution was a form of denial, a kind of defense mechanism to allay the anxiety that travels with cancer. But I didn't view it that way at the time. Moreover, for the better part of two and a half years following my diagnoses, I didn't have weekly scheduled medical appointments or a daily regimen of targeted pills to bombard me with reminders that I was being treated for cancer. After the surgical excision of the bladder tumor, I was on a three-month appointment schedule for cystoscopies and meetings with my urologist.

During this period of wait-and-see dormancy, I was mostly asymptomatic, aside from some moderate fatigue and gradual weight loss. I thus thought I could keep my illness sealed away in the backstage of my consciousness by making a deliberate effort not to treat it as an object of attention. A good idea perhaps, but also an improbable one given the intersection of the character of consciousness and the physiologically and psychologically obtrusive nature of cancer. Given that consciousness entails awareness of oneself, of one's thoughts, feelings, impulses, and even wakefulness, as well as awareness of one's surroundings, a bewildering clutter of thoughts can flit in and out of one's consciousness during the day, and even when asleep.[1] In one moment you may be focused on an exercise routine, but that focus may be suddenly disrupted by a question posed by a co-exerciser asking about a sporting event or new TV series. Minutes later you check your watch and notice that it is 5:45 p.m. You begin thinking about dinner and what you might eat. And so it goes.

Even if I tried not to think about it, I found myself investigating the nature of the cancers I'd been diagnosed with, perhaps accentuating my anxiety about my two cancers and their relationship, if any. Through a series of appointments with my CLL/SLL oncologist from late 2017 to the present—coupled with my lived experience negotiating the illness and the relevant materials I accessed through the CLL Society website or on my own—I gradually acquired an understanding of CLL and SLL. By "gradual," I reference the stepwise way in which I learned about my cancers, with each new change in the course of the illness and associated complications generating new questions and a reach for relevant information.

In a nutshell, I came to understand that CLL and SLL are related types of blood cancer of the lymphatic system, which is charged with fighting disease and infection throughout the body. They develop when white blood cells—B lymphocytes—change and grow out of control into B cell lymphomas. Together with T cell lymphomas,[2] they comprise non-Hodgkin lymphomas (NHL), which, according to the National Cancer Institute's 2025 estimates, is the eighth most frequent cancer in the US, albeit a relatively uncommon one, adding to just 4 percent of all cancers and three percent of cancer deaths.[3] Still, NHL accounts for around 90 percent of all lymphomas, with the B cell variety accounting for the vast majority. Among the ten or so B cell lymphomas, CLL/SLL is the third most common, with around twenty-four thousand new cases estimated for 2025 in the US.[4]

Normal B lymphocytes—which Siddhartha Mukherjee dubs "the defending cell"—help fight infection by creating antibodies that bind themselves to pathogens to keep them from entering and infecting normal cells.[5] But when altered via malignancy, B lymphocytes abnormally reproduce and crowd out normal blood cells, making it difficult for the body to fight infection. It's why those who have either CLL or SLL, as well as those suffering from other types of lymphoma, are immunocompromised.

Among the different types of B cell lymphomas, CLL and SLL are counted as one type because they are essentially the same. Analogically, they can be thought of as identical twin cancers since they are indistinguishable except for their frequency and locus.[6] According to my oncologist, whose research focused principally on their analysis and treatment, they generate the same symptoms such as fever, night sweats, and weight loss, and they respond to the same treatments.

There are two differences, however, but not in their structure or microscopic, genetic fingerprints. One difference is in their frequency. As my oncologist explained once while discussing my case, "Your SLL is very rare in comparison to CLL. There are only about three SLL cases for every one hundred CLL cases." The other difference is where they cluster in the lymphatic and blood circulatory systems: CLL cancer cells are found mainly in the blood and bone marrow; SLL cancer cells are mostly in the lymph nodes and the spleen. It's that difference that explains in part why my white blood cell count was always within the normal range while my lymph nodes were enlarged to various degrees. And it's that locational difference in the cancer's manifestation that accounts for the difference in the last word of their three-word names: chronic lymphocytic *leukemia* versus small lymphocytic *lymphoma*. It took me a while to grasp that difference, but once I did, I had a better understanding of my SLL and was better able to explain it to others when they asked.

Still, I was curious if there were signs of the CLL that I'd missed or disregarded before the blood in the urine exposed it. Clearly there was one. In the spring of 2017, a full six months before the initial diagnosis, I felt a lymph node in my neck that was larger than usual and scheduled an ultrasound. The results revealed slight enlargement, but apparently not sufficiently alarming to dig deeper. Swollen lymph nodes are not uncommon, as they are usually a temporary and harmless signal that your body is fighting an infection like the flu or a cold. So the examining radiologist let it go, as did I.

Such diagnostic indeterminacy was also at play in relation to a couple of other medical issues that surfaced right around the time of my initial diagnosis and beyond. One was cardiological, the other was gastrointestinal, both of which created more diagnostic uncertainty.

In the months preceding my diagnosis, I had had trouble initiating my cardiovascular exercise routines, whether lap swimming or power walking. I had no shortness of breath or chest agitation, only low energy. When I began the routines, I felt like a big rig truck trying to find the right gear to climb a long hill. Once I found the gear, however, I was able to complete the routines, although not as energetically as I had in the past. I found this somewhat concerning, so I contacted a cardiologist about these concerns and he scheduled a stress echocardiogram. Coincidentally, it was scheduled on the Tuesday of the week I was hospitalized for excision of the bladder tumor and a lymph node. The stress test was canceled, since the two cancer surgeries were understandably more urgent. Several months later, still thinking there might be a heart issue, I rescheduled the stress echo. The results were unremarkable, suggesting that the alteration in my energy level when engaging in cardiovascular exercise was probably due to the SLL-induced fatigue rather than to some cardio malfunction.

As I was confronted with reduced energy—one of the several symptoms linked to CLL/SLL—I wasn't able to pinpoint a definitive diagnostic connection because of the generality of fatigue as a medical complaint and the fact it was still the only pronounced symptom I had experienced. After my diagnosis, I suspected that my fatigue was due to the simmering, albeit dormant, SLL. The problem with fatigue as a symptom of any illness is that it can be symptomatic of a host of illnesses as well as a traveling companion of aging. When I mentioned the fatigue to my oncologist sometime in 2019, she said, "Well, you are in your seventies, and people tend to experience more fatigue when they get older, especially when they are physically active like you." Fatigue by itself, then, is rarely definitively symptomatic of any singular ailment, especially when one feels fine, as I did. I even found myself telling a few family members and friends, when they asked about my cancer, "It must be the most genial cancer one can have. It's had little, if any, disruptive effect on my daily life up to this point other than some fatigue."

I had also experienced lower gastrointestinal irregularity and agitation in the months prior to my diagnosis. In May 2017, for example, during a two-week trip to Northern Ireland to learn more about "the Troubles" and the twentieth anniversary of the peace resolution, I surprisingly found myself experiencing lower-intestinal agitation, so much that I missed a couple daily exploratory outings in order to stay sequestered in the Belfast hotel, attributing my symptoms to something I had eaten in a local pub. Later that spring was when I had an ultrasound showing the slightly enlarged lymph nodes in my neck, but neither my physicians nor I made a hypothetical connection between the two issues at the time.

Such diagnostic indeterminacy is not uncommon. For a number of years, *The New York Times Sunday Magazine* featured a section chronicling medical diagnostic enigmas.[7] The stories suggested to me that diagnostics is a hydra-headed process. It is often confronted with various conundrums and is usually contingent on the input of the examining clinical physicians, the diagnostic technicians who read the results of the MRIs and CT scans, and the patients themselves, whose level of engagement in the process can vary considerably. Most of the time there is overlapping agreement among the various sets of actors in the process; other times there are doubts and questions among one or more set of players about a proffered diagnosis or some aspect of it. In my case, for example, the CLL/SLL diagnosis was certain, but its severity and staging over time, as well as its treatment and initiation, were unclear and undefined.

Clearly I got caught up in a common diagnostic trap wherein my initial sense that the two issues were rooted in the cardiovascular and gastrointestinal systems functioned as an anchoring bias, deflecting consideration of the role my evolving SLL may have played as the causal determinant.[8] I realized that a patient's inclinations are unlikely to be weighted heavily in most diagnostic decisions, but in this case no physician offered any countermanding opinions. Such, it seems, is the twisting character of the hydra-headed diagnostic process, something I would sense even more acutely once I entered the clinical trial. Throughout all of this, I couldn't get a firm handle on what to make of what I was experiencing or how to feel about it other than being somewhat fearful. An overlapping puzzlement was how to weigh the dual diagnosis and subsequent experiences in relation to other aspects of my life. I grappled with how much I should let the cancers overwhelm or subjugate my other concerns and obligations. *How salient should the cancer diagnoses be, and what should I make of them in the context of work, family, and friendship? Should they be frontstage or backstage? Do the conditions and kindred circumstances impose themselves regardless of my preferences or intent? And does its weightiness or salience fluctuate?*

Its weightiness notwithstanding, I wasn't inclined to announce my cancer or put it center stage. There were times, however, when a doctor's appointment or eventual treatments and the day-after side effects such as fatigue or an irritable bowel would force my hand, requiring me to use my condition as an acceptable excuse for missing a scheduled social encounter or volunteer obligation. After my diagnosis, I had no clear, comfortable guidelines as to how to negotiate such situations, which led to feelings of anomie and its attendant ambiguity.

Anomie is a long-standing sociological concept referring to a condition of normlessness in which the traditional guidelines no longer hold, leading to a sense of disorientation and disconnection among members of the impacted society or group. Sociologists generally think of it as a property of an enveloping social structure and culture, but they also apply it at the individual level, denoting bewildering confusion when one feels adrift due to the loss or absence of familiar or clarifying moorings.[9] This is how I often felt—and continued to feel—throughout my cancer journey.

This sense of anomic ambiguity, as well as not knowing how much to allow cancer to intrude on my psychological or social life, fed into and fueled my ongoing uncertainty and anxiety about the prominence my cancer would or should play in terms of my identity. Sometimes unanticipated breaks in one's routines call forth a new identity, with a resultant reshuffling of the salience of one's various identities. Illness is especially likely to do that, particularly when it generates changes in one's physical appearance, modifies one's physical and mental capabilities, or leads to unforeseen absences. But, as noted earlier, being issued a "new identity card" upon entering the kingdom of illness doesn't mean it has to be used as the principal peg on which one's identity is hung.

Given these intersecting feelings of anomic ambiguity and identity confusion, it is not surprising that my imagination was also in play through several repeated dreams involving the loss of my internal geographic compass, neutralizing my ability to find my way to some destination. Sometimes I was in an unfamiliar city and unable to find my way back to my hotel; other times I couldn't recall how to get back to a campus lecture hall; and still at other times I was unable to get myself to a train station or airport on time for a scheduled departure home. Dreams involving the loss of one's geographic markers and way are fairly common, and probably among the most easily interpreted, according to neuroscientist Rahul Jandial's book on dreams, because of their connection to current or impending stresses.[10] Given the odyssey-like character of cancer and the associated uncertainty of its prognosis, it is hardly surprising, then, that I would have dreams wherein I was lost because I couldn't find my way.

Perhaps not coincidentally, the dream-based loss of my geographic compass overlapped with a mid-February 2020 flight Roberta and I took to St. Louis to meet the family of my son's fiancée. Little did we know that would be the last time we would step into an airport terminal and board a plane for over three years due to the confluence of a number of unforeseen *Odyssey*-like obstacles, including a new virus spreading across the globe.

CHAPTER 4

Pandemic Challenges and Medical Jolts

Everybody knows that pestilences have a way of recurring in the world; yet somehow we find it hard to believe in ones that crash down on our heads from a blue sky. There have been as many plagues as wars in history; yet always plagues and wars take people equally by surprise.

—ALBERT CAMUS[1]

The World Health Organization (WHO) identified COVID-19 as a Public Health Emergency of International Concern on January 31, 2020, with the US Secretary of the Department of Health and Human Services doing the same.[2] But the case incidence and spread had not yet prompted parallel concern across the world among politicians and citizens, including ourselves. The fire alarm had been sounded, but apparently not loud enough, as it seemed to have fallen on deaf ears.

We may not have made the trip to St. Louis had we caught wind of the warning. And we were not alone, as many other travelers didn't seem to have heard it. Being sociological field-workers, Roberta and I are sensitized to overhearing the conversations of others—eavesdropping it might be called—but in our flights to and from St. Louis we didn't hear any anxious talk about this novel virus. And we had no discussion of it when meeting and visiting with our son's future in-laws. Nor did it come up over a breakfast with a former student of Roberta's who had recently received her master's degree in public health from Washington University in St. Louis. Clearly a good many folks acted as if they were unaware of or indifferent to the dual public health emergency warnings, ourselves included.

But within a short time after our return, the virus began to do what viruses are biologically programmed to do when they encounter vulnerable and ill-prepared host populations: They bind themselves to the hosts, multiply, and spread. And this is what SARS-CoV-2—the virus that causes COVID-19—did. It began to spread like a windswept prairie fire. So much so that on March 11 the World Health Organization declared a pandemic, with the Trump administration issuing a national emergency a few days later.

In anticipation of my birthday that coming week, Roberta had made a dinner reservation for all ten immediate family members in the early evening of Sunday, March 15. However, given the louder clanging of the alarm bells, Roberta and I decided to err on the side of caution and cancel and reschedule the celebration for some time after the threat of the virus had subsided. Little did we or anyone else know that it would be three years down the road. Canceling the reservation a few days ahead appeared to be the right call as states began issuing mandatory stay-at-home orders to curtail the virus's rapid spread. By April, about half of the world's population was under some form of governmental lockdown directive, and the world had come to an anomic standstill.

One of the ironies of the pandemic is that while it linked the world together in the global threat posed by COVID-19, it also nurtured a sociocultural and political virus that would accentuate our divisions and deepen our reciprocal animosities. This divisive virus was not new, as it had been seeded for some time.[3] But the viral pandemic watered and cultivated that divisive seedbed, which manifested itself in anti-lockdown and anti-mask protests, a spiraling antivaccine movement, and the disinformation and conspiracism that fueled and animated them.[4]

At the forefront, at least initially, were the anti-lockdown protests. Populated by anti-maskers, long-gun-toting militia types, flag-flying supporters of the Confederacy, antivaccination adherents, and some folks understandably pressed to get back to work, these protests popped up especially in the capitals of states where governors had issued shelter-in-place orders, like Lansing, Michigan; Madison, Wisconsin; and Sacramento, California. Unlike the massive, widespread Black Lives Matter protests in the wake of George Floyd's murder, they were another outcropping of the politicization of the COVID mitigation efforts, including the shaming of public officials advocating mask wearing, the rendering of conspiratorial claims that the virus's incidence and escalating death count were exaggerated, and that the pandemic was manufactured and sold to China by the Obama Administration or was a hoax promulgated by the "deep state" in order to derail then President Trump's bid for a second term.[5] It was in this unsettling, divisive context that we all had to negotiate the pandemic.

For me, however, as well as others living with cancer, there was the additional complication of being immunocompromised. Even though I was still in the "watch and wait" stage of the disease, I was reminded by my oncologist and her nurse practitioner to continue to take extra precautions to guard against COVID. I can't say that the precautions we took set us apart from others, but it was clear that we were guarded when we ventured out. When we went grocery shopping, for example, we rose around six a.m. so we could ready ourselves to arrive at the market between seven and seven thirty in hopes that there would be a scant number of shoppers. And when we arrived, we made sure we were well-covered and prepared, with face masks, baseball caps, throwaway plastic gloves, and a detailed shopping list. No second-guessing or asking each other while shopping what we were supposed to get. The aim was to get in and out as quickly as possible, transfer the purchased items from the cart to our grocery bags in the trunk, and drive the short distance home, all within about forty-five minutes, with Roberta wiping off each item as I unpacked the bags. This was the customary shopping ritual we followed for the first several months of the pandemic. Did it shield us from the novel virus? Who knows for certain, although it seems reasonable to surmise that the measures taken may have mattered, since neither of us had COVID until almost two years later.

Inasmuch as lockdown ordinances were followed, Roberta and I were far from alone in being grounded and homebound. We had a lot of company from a significant proportion of the world. Evidence was everywhere: in flight reductions, which were almost triple those in the wake of the 9/11 attacks;[6] in the reduction of vehicle miles traveled, with a 75 percent drop in traffic in college towns, the large urban areas of the northeast, and in California's coastal cities;[7] and in eating and drinking outside the home, with the restaurant and bar industry brought to a halt.[8] Even in our neighborhood, which has walking paths and nearby trails, a greater number of neighbors could be seen walking than prior to the lockdown, more food deliveries were evident, and, for the most part, cars remained in the garages or outdoor parking spots.

Early on Easter Sunday morning, Roberta and I got a keen sense of the extent to which our geographic portion of the world was sheltering in place. I was awakened around 2:30 a.m. with severe, piercing pain in my abdomen—a 6 to 7 on a 10-point scale. Advil wouldn't touch it.

Even though I was still in the wait-and-watch stage of the CLL/SLL, I was certain the pain was symptomatic of its activation or, even more worrisome, of the occurrence of some other cancer in the abdominal area, perhaps even metastasis. After trying to wait it out for about two hours, Roberta drove me to the emergency room. We were struck by the eerie emptiness of the freeways. In the twelve-mile drive on three different freeways to the hospital, we counted no more than a half dozen vehicles. Roberta, who grew up in the Los Angeles metroplex and had lived most of her life in Southern California, remarked, "I have never seen so few cars on the freeway." It was chillingly uncanny, like right out of a dystopian movie.

Clearly, people were adhering to the stay-at-home orders, but not so much because of the generalized goodwill of citizens sheltering in place. There simply wasn't anyplace to go due to the mandated closure of most businesses and places of work except those deemed as "essential," such as grocery and drug stores. Most folks didn't have much choice.

The large hospital complex was eerily quiet, too, in spite of the presence of a huge tent that now stretched across the front of the building and a smaller tent for accessing the emergency unit. We pulled into an emergency parking space and went to what appeared to be the emergency tent. A uniformed security officer said that only unaccompanied patients were allowed to enter. Roberta said she would wait for me in the parked car in hopes that she wouldn't be sent out of the area, and we would keep in touch via cell phone, both of us hoping that I could be treated and sent home. The last thing we wanted was for me to be admitted to the hospital, presumably full of COVID patients, and where no visitors were allowed at that time. But luckily, that was not the case. I received an intravenous dose of morphine that alleviated my pain, and a CT scan revealed diverticulosis rather than cancer in the stomach or any adjacent organs. Relieved, of course, but not disabused of the possibility that my variant of lymphoma wasn't implicated in some way. Indeed, the CT report noted "lymphadenopathy throughout the abdomen and pelvis," which had "increased from the prior exam." Even though the report pointed to diverticulosis as the principal source of the pain, cancer was still on my mind. Such is the nature of cancer consciousness, often prompting the worse-case scenarios.

These fluctuating thoughts aside, as the lockdown wore on, so did the impatience of a growing number of citizens. Our sense from talking with neighbors, family, and friends—often via Zoom—was that for most people the restlessness manifested itself in grumbling about the indefinite duration of the lockdown. During a daily morning walk in the middle of April, Roberta and I passed the home of a former neighbor. He was bent over trimming some bushes in front of his house. We stopped and asked how he was doing. He turned around and said, "I'm bored. I can't take much more of this staying in."

"Yeah, it is tough," I replied, "but better than getting the virus."

"This lockdown is killing the economy," he said. "Poverty kills people too."

Roberta and I acknowledged all three concerns, saying that there were trade-offs, wished him a good day, and walked on, commenting to each other that his crusty remarks weren't surprising given our familiarity with his disposition.

But we also mused that it was understandable that comments and gripes like our neighbor's were becoming more commonplace as the lockdown persisted. Like millions of others, we also looked forward to the lockdown's cessation. We were tired of seeing our adult children and grandchildren from a distance, first through drive-bys, then by visits in their backyards or our garage with plenty of distance between us, as when one of our daughters visited on the first Saturday of May, a month and half into the lockdown. On her way she picked up lunch from one of my favorite burger shops. It was a real treat as we sat face-to-face, albeit at opposite ends of the garage with the door open. But even more of a treat was simply sitting there and talking. It was so nice to talk in person rather than via the cell phone or Zoom. We talked about family, about working virtually, about politics, and about surviving the quarantine. However, what we talked about was less important than that we were together in the same physical space just talking. We replayed this same ritual a week and a half later when we visited the home of another daughter, sitting outside at the end of a picnic table while she, her husband, and our granddaughter were spaced around their firepit, fifteen feet away. We celebrated another granddaughter's eighteenth birthday under the shade of an awning her dad had constructed on their front yard, taking care to eat separately and clapping hands to extinguish candles rather than blowing them out. And then again, on Mother's Day, our son and his fiancée visited. We sat at opposite ends of our open garage eating the lunch they brought and talking about their forthcoming wedding and negotiating the pandemic.

There was an understandable awkwardness to such gatherings. In reflecting on these encounters, I remarked to Roberta that I don't think I have ever experienced a time where the substance of conversation felt so secondary or irrelevant to simply being physically and emotionally present with those with whom we were interacting. When we said goodbye on these and other such occasions with family, I felt a bit sad, perhaps even depressed. I missed the physical connection with my children and grandchildren. I wanted to hug them but yet was reluctant to do so because the SLL rendered me severely immunocompromised, and they were equally cautious about passing something on to me.

Because of the lack of regular face-to-face interaction, of physical contact among family and friends, some individuals within our broader social circles came up with innovative ways to bring people together virtually via Zoom gatherings. Such was the case with a Friday night Zoom gathering that began early in the lockdown stage of the pandemic and continues now as an almost ritualized gathering. The Zoom gathering was organized by a couple we knew well, but we didn't initially know any of the other participants, who were acquaintances of the organizing couple. These weekly virtual gatherings usually included ten to fifteen participants, and were anchored temporally in the same two-hour Friday evening time slot, between seven and nine o'clock. In the first hour, we socialized and caught up on each other's lives; and in the second hour, we played Codenames—a board game that can be played virtually by four or more participants split into two teams in which the players guess words in a five-by-five grid based on the word clues from their teammates. Roberta and I subsequently learned that many of our fellow participants knew each other in advance of the first gathering. But they were all strangers to us, initially. In time, however, a new set of friendships blossomed during the weekly virtual social hour discussions. These emergent friendships were nurtured in no small part by the range and depth of our discussions. We learned about each other's biographic pasts, professional work life, families, health and medical issues, travels, and leisure pursuits. We also talked about politics and religion, and various timely social issues, such as homelessness, health insurance, and social inequality. Indeed, there was little in our lives or in the context of the time that wasn't germane for discussion.

Another anchored virtual group emerged in a similar unscripted, organic way at the outset of the pandemic. In the first several weeks of the lockdown I received an email from an acquaintance asking if I would be interested in joining a weekday morning Zoom group to discuss and brainstorm ways to improve on tracking and assessing the spread of the pandemic, with the hopeful aim of deriving a useful analytical scheme that might be monetized. This small group included two retired pharmaceutical executives (one of whom was a physician), a former CFO for several companies, myself (presumably because of research I had conducted on the costs of homelessness for the county in which we lived), and the organizer, who was a PhD data analyst. Initially we met several times a week, but as the pandemic waned, so did the frequency of our meetings. We never did produce a scheme for predicting the spread of the pandemic that was an improvement on what already existed via the CDC and various university public health research initiatives. Nonetheless, we continued to meet on Friday mornings, usually for an hour, to catch up on what had transpired in our lives and the world during the previous week. And what began as an anchored analytical and monetizing project had transformed into a Friday morning virtual coffee-klatch among a small group of graying guys. As with the Codenames group, we checked on each other's well-being, families, and travels, and discussed current events locally and beyond. We also humored each other in a good way, finding or saying things that generated mutual laughter. I think we all came to understand that laughing together is an important variant of emotional support, no less so than empathizing with others or shedding tears together. The interpersonal connections spilled over into other places to varying degrees for the members, but the virtually generated friendships remained viable, judging from the ongoing durability of the Friday morning Zoom meetings.

As the first pandemic year wore on, COVID not only reconfigured relationships but also the "doing" of everyday tasks, including medical exams, complicating and changing our medical encounters. Before the pandemic, Roberta had joined me in the exam room, asking questions, jotting notes, and providing the physicians with important contexts. But now, with the new COVID protocols, she wasn't allowed to come in with me. This was discombobulating in the anomic ambiguity way since she had been with me at every appointment. So now I didn't have my co-observer and interrogator. Metaphorically, it now felt like I was driving the stagecoach or big truck without my reliable shotgun rider beside me. Initially, she sat downstairs in the waiting room of the building and participated via cell phone. Further tightening of the protocols prohibited nonpatients from entering the building, but we compensated by keeping our cell phones on so she could sit in the car high in the parking structure and still ask follow-up questions and get clarification as if she were in the examining room.

Unlike the millions of others making adjustments to the pandemic's anomic ambiguity, Roberta and I had to be especially vigilant because of my being immunocompromised, especially as I continued to be in a "watch and wait" status for my SLL. My heightened vulnerability captured our attention until that summer, when encounters with two unexpected cancers other than SLL shifted our focus from negotiating the pandemic and its amplified threat to dealing with these jolts.

The first jolt was the appearance of a growing and irregular-shaped lesion on the tragus (the small, pointed bump in front of the ear canal) of my right ear, which sent me to the dermatologist for a biopsy. The lab report wasn't definitive but suggested pleomorphic dermal sarcoma—a rare, aggressive skin cancer with metastatic potential.[9] Recalling what my oncologist had said about skin cancer being the only cancer that CLL/SLL is most likely to trigger, perhaps I shouldn't have been surprised. But I was, probably because of concern about the activation of my SLL, the ongoing threat of COVID, and the passing of a sister-in-law twenty-five years earlier due to a rare soft tissue sarcoma.

In any case, given this concerning diagnostic tilt of the biopsy report, I was scheduled several weeks later for Mohs surgery. The surgery involves removal of one layer of impacted tissue at a time for immediate microscopic inspection for the cancer, with the process repeated until excision of all the cancerous tissue. For me, this process took four and a half hours, entailing removal of four layers of the tumor but without fully clean margins because of evidence of what the lab report called "perineural involvement."

This meant that the probable sarcoma had invaded and annexed tissue surrounding connecting nerves, increasing the prospect of metastasis. Accordingly, the dermatologist, in consultation with the department tumor team, referred me to interventional radiology, which recommended thirty daily radiation treatments to neutralize the prospect of neural metastasis. Clearly, Roberta and I weren't enthusiastic about the twenty-five-mile freeway round trip five days a week for six weeks for radiation therapy that involved lying flat and being slid into a large linear accelerator while wearing a fitted protective helmet. This daily afternoon procedure, along with the travel, consumed most of the afternoon for a month and a half, as well as leaving the right side of my face with an irritating radiation burn for yet another month or so. But what viable alternatives were there when the Mohs lab report indicates perineural involvement by the sarcoma?

In addition to the sarcoma on the right ear, three more skin cancers were identified—two squamous cell cancers, with one on my lower left arm and the other on my right cheek, and an ill-defined carcinoma on my left cheek. The temporal clustering of these skin cancers with the occurrence of the SLL (even though it was in abeyance for much of the time) would suggest a robust causal link, especially since it is estimated that CLL/SLL victims are five to eight times more likely to have skin cancers. But other factors were at work, such as age and long-term sun exposure due to lap swimming three times a week for over forty years in the often sun-drenched landscapes of Austin, Texas; Tucson, Arizona; and Southern California, where most pools are outdoors. Given the intersection of these contributing factors, it seems reasonable to conclude that the skin cancers were overdetermined, meaning that any one of probable causal agents—the sun exposure, my age, and the SLL, among other factors—could have precipitated their occurrence. In any case, after the signs of radiation burn around the ear had diminished, the only visible residue of the surgery and treatment was the disappearance of the tragus, which seemed functionless to me other than serving to hold my AirPods in place when walking and listening to music. From then on, I could only use one AirPod when stretching, walking, or lifting weights because the other one would invariably fall out. But that struck me as a small price to pay for neutralization of the sarcoma skin cancer.

In between the Mohs surgery in June for the sarcoma on my right ear and the radiation therapy in August, I experienced another cancer jolt: the recurrence of bladder cancer. A July cystoscopy revealed two cancerous polyps and a stressed-looking bladder. Here again, I was somewhat surprised because the cystoscopies I had been having every three months since the tumor excision in October 2017 were clear and clean. Roberta, too, looked closely at the cystoscopy monitor, this time with alarm. On the other hand, I had learned that bladder cancer tends to recur, with an estimated one-year recurrence rate between 15 and 61 percent, and a five-year recurrence rate from 31 to 78 percent.[10] So I shouldn't have been too surprised, especially with the odds of recurrence apparently increasing over time. But knowing the statistical odds does little to soften the news that there has been a relapse. Hearing that the cancer has returned is invariably a shock. A jolt to the psyche if not to one's resolve.

My urologist was confidently reassuring, however, explaining not only that the cancerous lesions could be removed, but that he was going to perform the surgery via a blue light cystoscopy technology, which enables clearer identification of cancerous tumors and distinguishes them from healthy bladder tissue. Once the lesions were excised and the surgery completed, the bladder was injected with a dose of chemo for good measure, and I was released shortly thereafter with a cancer-free bladder. The development of new technologies, like blue light cystoscopies, has advanced the control of bladder cancer, but the key, as I learned firsthand, is ongoing monitoring via scheduled cystoscopies and patient vigilance. The urologist, like the dermatologist, was in the attack mode.

These two cancerous jolts might be thought of as setbacks, but that's not how we or the relevant specialists approached them. Rather, we saw them as flare-ups that were part and parcel of the two cancers, flare-ups that could be doused by applying the appropriate antidotes as soon as possible. I had read that CLL/SLL increased one's vulnerability to some other cancers, but neither the reemergent bladder cancer nor the sarcoma skin cancer was diagnostically associated with the SLL, at least not directly. Even though my oncologist reminded me, "It isn't a direct precipitant of any cancer other than skin cancers," I remained curious about the likelihood of my bladder cancer being a secondary one.

If these summer jolts weren't enough, I started having symptoms reminding me of the SLL lying in wait in my body. Foremost were the night sweats I experienced for four weeks in July. My oncologist, as well as the various literature I had read about CLL/SLL symptoms, had forewarned me about these night sweats, but this is not to say that every CLL or SLL sufferer experiences these sweats. But I did, and they were drenching, often forcing me to change my T-shirt three to five times a night. In their anticipation, I even began piling up several T-shirts on the bureau beside our bed before calling it a night. But, just as suddenly as the night sweats came on, they vanished. What triggered the night sweats and their cessation is unclear; there are any number of factors, in isolation or combination. It probably was the SLL, but the warmer summer nights might have also sparked them, even though we had an overhead fan. As with many symptomatic conditions, the animating causes can be difficult to identify. My oncologist made this clear several times when I asked her "why this or that" with respect to my SLL, and she would respond candidly, "We just don't know." In any case, since there were no other alarming symptoms or evidence of disease progression, I remained in the watch-and-wait status.

At this time, too, I started experiencing lower gastrointestinal irregularity and agitation. Several visits to the gastroenterologist failed to yield a diagnosis, but he offered a Band-Aid solution: Take two Pepcid a day and an Imodium as frequently as needed. This was somewhat helpful as a stopgap measure, even though the causal determinant of the issue was still open-ended.

Life went on this way through the remainder of 2020 and into the winter months of 2021, with no significant changes in the daily routines we established in the wake of the shelter-in-place orders. In fact, Roberta and I almost took those routines for granted: limited outings beyond the home to nearby grocery stores, the local pharmacy, the residences of our children, and to the numerous medical visits, while being diligent about mask wearing and social distancing. Like most folks within the pandemic context, we had settled into a kind of new normal. We didn't do so enthusiastically, but we were conscientious about continuing with the precautionary measures we had been pursuing, especially since we presumed that they had effectively mitigated our exposure to the virus up to this point. An equally important consideration was that older adults—those sixty-five and up—were strikingly more susceptible to serious illness and dying from COVID-19 than younger individuals.[11] Since we were in that vulnerable age category and I was immunosuppressed, we had no problem sticking with the recommended safeguards including a new one that emerged in the spring of 2021: COVID vaccination.

Given that we welcomed the availability of these vaccines, we jumped at the opportunity to get the shots at their first availability. We immediately investigated where and how to get our vaccinations and learned that a temporary vaccination center would be set up in one of the remote Disneyland parking lots, with priority given to older people. We knew the hours but didn't know how to get in, how it would be organized, or what to look for. Local newspapers warned that there would be long lines and we imagined that standing in them would be difficult, so we borrowed an old wheelchair from a neighbor in case we wanted to take turns sitting. But when we arrived at the site, we saw a collection of folding chairs in the parking lot.

The whole vaccination scene was clearly organized, but was still overlaid with the fog of anomic ambiguity. Hundreds of people were there, with winding lines of parking cars and people waiting in line for their shots, asking each other about what was going on. Roberta and I waited about two hours before getting to the front of the line where people were divided up by age and directed to one of several large tents. We may have arrived a little sooner once Roberta began pushing me in the wheelchair, as we thought pushing an empty chair might look strange. We showed our IDs, were given our shots, and were issued our vaccination cards. Afterward, the nurses directed us to sit and wait to see if there were any complications. We did wait, but not the full twenty minutes since we didn't feel any aftereffects. Somehow we got separated as we returned to the car—I was pushing the empty chair, which I'm sure looked odd, as did the whole anomic scene.

Vaccination against COVID, however, provided only a temporary sense of relief. As spring transitioned into summer, my condition began to slide downward, at first gradually and then precipitously. The time of only watching and waiting had clearly come to an end, and I took another uncertain step forward on my *Odyssey* journey.

CHAPTER 5

Joining the Clinical Trial

I think there's a lot of reluctance about clinical trials because we've done a very bad job of educating the public on what a clinical trial means and how important it is and how the only way to learn with this disease is to participate. If we don't partner with patients, then the discipline is lost. The partnership with patients is absolutely critical.

—SIDDHARTHA MUKHERJEE[1]

Initially, I noticed a decline in my endurance when exercising. Having been a longtime lap swimmer—averaging a mile swim three times per week for forty-some years—I tried to maintain my long-standing exercise routine, consisting of fast-walking on the days in between my swims, along with light weightlifting. I did so because I thought it was physically beneficial, as suggested by recent research at the Memorial Sloan Kettering Cancer Center indicating that "regular exercise during cancer treatment appears to act like a good double whammy. It reduces the risk of dying from certain cancers. And the 'side effect' of exercise is actually helpful because it reduces the risk of dying from causes other than cancer, such as heart disease."[2] But equally important for me were the psychological effects. One was the feeling of well-being that comes from the production of endorphins, our brain's feel-good neurotransmitters, via exercise. And this is particularly true of aerobic exercise, such as rowing, swimming, and running; hence, the so-called "runner's high." Not surprisingly, I always felt better after swimming for forty-five to fifty minutes or more, even when slogging through the water in the wake of cancer's advance. There were other payoffs as well; I felt more relaxed and less anxiety in the hours after swimming or walking. I suspect that my push to maintain my exercise routine was a key factor in mitigating the prospect of more severe depression than the intermittent, fleeting bouts I experienced. Now, however, not only did I struggle to complete three-quarters of a mile, but also my pace was much slower. Even when my cancer was progressing and my energy and stamina were waning, I would still give it a shot, even if my walking pace had slowed to a near–nursing home shuffle. I simply didn't have the energy or stamina.

Some of the other regular swimmers noticed the change in my pace and distance, asking me, "What's going on?" Some neighbors asked the same question about my walking. Whereas I had been walking at a pretty good clip, around a sixteen- to seventeen-minute mile, now I moped along, with the pace seemingly slowing every couple of weeks, to where, by the middle of the summer, I was lumbering along at best, laboring to lift and move one foot after the other. As one neighbor, who could observe me from his living room window walking up and down the street, remarked, "I could monitor the progression of your cancer by just watching you walk." My withering energy and stamina were, of course, emblematic of the severe fatigue that usually accompanies cancer's advance. But what I found so alarming was how quickly and how much my energy had dissipated, especially since I considered myself to be in reasonably good cardiovascular condition. Now, however, I was running on fumes.

Equally troubling was the corresponding distension of my abdomen. Being a lap swimmer, I didn't have a protruding belly. But now I looked like I had been cultivating one over the course of a few months. My children noticed it, as did Roberta, who once commented, "You look like you have a beer belly." Even when pushing myself to swim, some of the co-swimmers remarked to Roberta about my noticeably expanding abdomen.

The acute distension was also evident to my oncologist and the nurse practitioner, and not only visibly. When they palpated my abdomen, they felt enlarged lymph nodes or clusters of nodes and an inflated spleen, both conspicuous markers of disease progression. Their observations were consistent with a late spring CT scan, which showed extensive abdominal and pelvic swollen lymph nodes (lymphadenopathy). Based on these radiological results and clinical observations, coupled with my generalized withering energy, I was clearly well past the watch-and-wait plateau.

The cancer's progression both surprised and shocked me. It was surprising since I had thought, apparently naively, that I would get lucky and be among the 30 percent or so of CLL/SLL victims whose cancers remain dormant and never require treatment.[3] And I was shocked by how quickly it had progressed, reactivating the fear of the downward slide that occupied my thoughts in my first days in the hospital in 2017.

Another round of CT scans in mid-July highlighted its urgency and fueled my fears. Like the earlier scan, it noted "diffuse innumerable bulky lymphadenopathy in the abdomen and pelvis," but with the lymph nodes still increasing in size. Normal lymph nodes are the size of a pea, usually measuring less than a half inch across, which makes them close to one centimeter. Nodes that are larger are generally considered abnormal.[4] In my case, the nodes in my abdomen and pelvic area were extraordinarily large, with some measuring as much as 10 x 8 cm and 10.7 x 5.9 cm. Given their size, the report indicated that many of the organs in the abdomen were not well visualized and that the nodes had a "mass effect"—that is, they pushed significantly on several of the organs. For example, the report stated that my kidneys were "displaced laterally," the small bowel loops were "displaced," and there was "mass effect on the sigmoid colon by enlarged pelvic lymph nodes." The abdominal wall and mesentery (the organ that attaches the intestines to the abdominal wall) were also swollen with fluid.

"Eureka," I said, when I read that. No wonder my abdomen was severely distended. No wonder I was experiencing gastrointestinal irregularity and agitation: Growing, enlarged lymph nodes had been pressing on my bowels. And no wonder my energy had waned; greedy cancer cells were cannibalizing it for their growth, division, and survival. While I never received definitive clinical confirmation of this likely causal connection, I was pretty convinced that was it. The SLL appeared to be the culprit behind it all, and it became clear that my SLL was now advanced and required aggressive treatment.

I was curious, though, as to why my doctors hadn't initiated treatment earlier, given the mounting indicators of the cancer's advance months earlier. In fact, in the spring of 2021, Roberta and I asked my oncologist and her nurse practitioner when my treatments might begin. They replied that although they recognized that my overall condition was worsening, it did not yet constitute an emergency. They also said that I hadn't gone into treatment earlier because of the uncertainty of the pandemic.

Indeed, concerns about the COVID-19 pandemic affected access and receipt of medical care across the country. In the first year and a half of the pandemic, there was considerable concern about decreasing patient exposure, particularly of those with preexisting conditions like cancer, and for retaining as many beds as possible for anticipated influxes in COVID cases. Some hospitals—including ours—even assembled tent wards on the hospital grounds to accommodate the flood of COVID patients. Consequently, a good many citizens across the country postponed or avoided health care, or simply weren't able to get it. As early as June 20, 2020, a CDC study reported that "41% of US adults had delayed or avoided medical care including urgent or emergency care (12%) and routine care (32%)."[5] My case fell into that category; in fact, in late July, my oncologist said, "We would have begun treatment earlier had it not been for COVID." My experience was another illustration of the many ways in which COVID-19 intruded into all aspects of our lives during the height of the pandemic, affecting not only our daily lives and interaction patterns but also how we managed our medical conditions. Given its intrusive and unsettling reach, it could be argued that COVID shared with cancer its metastatic character, not necessarily physiologically but certainly sociologically and psychologically. Such postponement raises the vexing question of where the line is between what's emergency and what is elective and thus postponed. Whatever the answer, it seemed clear that I had now passed that line.

As the spring rolled into the summer and my condition continued to deteriorate to the point of a stage IV designation, it had become increasingly clear that treatment for which Roberta and I had been hoping was now mandated. The challenge was to find the best treatment option and initiate it as soon as possible.

Deciding on the optimal cancer treatment is never a simple decision, and numerous factors come into play. What is the type of cancer, and is it an initial or relapsed cancer? What are the treatment options for that particular cancer? What are the odds of the selected treatment controlling the cancer or driving it into remission? What are the most probable treatment side effects? Might some of these side effects be more deleterious than the cancer itself? And what about the costs of the treatment drugs and process? The questions one might ask about treatment decisions can sometimes seem interminable and daunting, with one answer prompting other vexing questions.

The factors that can affect one's treatment decisions are varied and generally cluster into three sets: physician and medical-based considerations, patient/personal matters, and contextual factors. The physician and medical-based factors include, for example, physician expertise and the range of treatment options, which have expanded over time from surgery to chemotherapy and radiation to targeted therapy, immunotherapy, stem cell or bone marrow therapy, and hormone therapy. Patient/personal factors include current health condition, previous medical issues and experiences (including those of immediate family members), presence of children, as well as age, gender, religion, and even political orientation, as we learned during the height of the pandemic. And contextual factors include financial status, medical insurance, caregiver availability, and proximity to relevant treatment facilities.[6] Not only are all of these factors relevant to treatment decisions, but how they are weighted can vary in innumerable ways among patients. And the initial decisions may often be subject to reassessment after the treatment and second-guessing down the road with changes in one's medical condition and encompassing context.

In the case of Judy's first encounter with breast cancer, she was initially confronted with the decision of whether to have a lumpectomy or mastectomy, and then whether to pursue chemotherapy and radiation or both. Even though the cancer was in its early stages and had not spread into her lymph nodes, she opted for the mastectomy and the combination of chemo and radiation. Her reasoning, with my support, was to pursue the treatment regimen which would increase the odds of seeing our three children—ranging in age from nine to fourteen at the time—graduate from high school, go to college, and become young adults. Although some friends and relatives initially questioned the decision to opt for the mastectomy over the less severe lumpectomy, it evidently was the right decision, as she remained cancer-free for fifteen years, during which time all three children graduated from college and one was married. She considered other factors, but clearly the presence of children weighed most heavily. Other couples, with or without children, may have made different calculations because of different configurations of factors and their relative salience to them. And that is the point: Treatment decisions are complicated given the array of factors that can impinge on them, and this is especially so when there is no surefire treatment option.

A few years earlier, while I was still in the watch-and-wait status, I had asked my oncologist about possible treatment options. She told me about ibrutinib, a relatively recent treatment regimen and standard-of-care targeted therapy option. She laid it out quite clearly during one appointment in spring 2019 when I was in the middle of retirement considerations, trying to decide whether to take my retirement savings as a pension or lump sum. I mentioned this quandary because my decision depended in part on my anticipated life expectancy. If I could expect only another five years or so, I certainly wasn't going to opt for the pension. Even though she didn't offer me any financial advice, which I didn't anticipate, she did tell me it was unlikely my SLL would kill me because frontline target therapies like ibrutinib could control it, but with the cautionary proviso that I would probably have to continue taking the drug, or some other parallel targeted therapy, daily for the remainder of my life. Indeed, a sister-in-law of my older sister had been diagnosed with CLL about five years prior to my diagnosis, and she was one of the early recipients of ibrutinib, and has been taking one or more pills daily and anticipates doing so for the rest of her life.

Known by its generic name and its market brand name Imbruvica, ibrutinib had come online around 2013 with the publication of the results of a clinical trial showing that it "was associated with a high frequency of durable remissions in patients with relapsed or refractory CLL and small lymphocytic lymphoma."[7] FDA approval followed in February 2014 for CLL/SLL patients who had received at least one prior treatment, with approval as a frontline treatment two years later for CLL/SLL patients regardless of treatment history. "This approval," according to executive vice president and chief scientific officer for the holding pharmaceutical company AbbVie, "represents a significant leap forward for patients diagnosed with CLL who may want to consider an alternative first-line treatment to traditional chemotherapy."[8] As an inhibitor of Bruton's tyrosine kinase (BTK)—an enzyme that is critical to the survival of malignant B lymphocytes[9]—ibrutinib works to prevent the spread and facilitate the death of malignant B cells in the blood or lymph nodes, short-circuiting the cancer-generating process that triggers CLL and SLL. As explained in the CLL Society website, "The CLL cells can no longer pick up the signals and so they leave the supportive and safe neighborhood of the nodes for the relative isolation of the blood stream where they eventually die off."[10]

Ibrutinib and other BTK inhibitors do this, unlike the chemotherapy option, by targeting the biochemical mechanisms that generate the growth and division of specific cancer cells rather than all cells. One way I grasped the difference between the two therapies is by drawing on the military distinction between "carpet" or saturation bombing and "target" or precision bombing. Like carpet bombing, chemotherapy generates devastating collateral damage, killing healthy, dividing cells as well as malignant cells, thus wreaking havoc system wide. Targeted therapy, in contrast, attacks the cancer cells without damaging or destroying the normal cells.

Because of this difference, the search for targeted therapies like ibrutinib has been described by Nathan Vardi, who chronicled the drug's research history in *For Blood and Money: Billionaires, Biotech, and the Quest for a Blockbuster Drug*, as "the holy grail of cancer drug development."[11]

But ibrutinib never fully clears the cancer from the blood, so patients "need to take a pill once a day, every day, for a long time—years."[12] Still, it was a "blood cancer game changer," indeed a lifesaver for hundreds of people suffering from CLL/SLL, but it wasn't a "magic bullet cure" since it rarely resulted in complete remissions.[13] And it was on the table for me as a treatment option.

Another possibility for me was a second-generation BTK inhibitor called acalabrutinib (Calquence). It received FDA approval as another frontline monotherapy for CLL/SLL in November 2019 and has been found to generate fewer and less severe adverse effects than ibrutinib, making it generally more tolerable and easily managed.[14] Had my only options been one of these two sister BTK inhibitors, in retrospect I probably would have selected acalabrutinib for reasons that should become clear in a subsequent chapter.

I never had to make that decision, because my oncologist presented to me a third alternative: a randomized, fifteen-month phase 3 clinical trial.

In contrast to phase 1 trials, which assess the safety of the treatment and the optimal way to give it, and phase 2 trials, which assess if the treatment works in affecting the targeted cancer, phase 3 trials assess whether some new treatment is more effective than the standard one. In this proffered phase 3 trial, the comparison was between the standard-of-care treatment—ibrutinib plus obinutuzumab—to a combination of that treatment plus the addition of venetoclax in the experimental arm of the study. Venetoclax and obinutuzumab, a monoclonal antibody infusion (sold under the brand name Gazyva), had been used and tested together but not previously in combination with ibrutinib in a large phase 3 trial.[15] These two targeted therapies work together, but in different ways. Obinutuzumab targets and binds to CD20 protein antigens on the surface of impacted B cells and blood cells, marking the malignant B cells for destruction by the immune system.[16] The study drug venetoclax, on the other hand, functions as an inhibitor by blocking a protein antigen called BCL-2 prominent in CLL/SLL cells, facilitating the death of the cancer cells. The objective of this phase 3 clinical trial was to assess the relative efficacy of the two standard-of-care control group drugs in combination with the experimental drug, venetoclax. Whereas previous clinical trials had shown ibrutinib—given alone or in combination with obinutuzumab—could produce a positive response rate, it was still a partial rather than a complete response. The aim, indeed hope of this clinical trial, was to see if the experimental triplet regimen could drive the CLL/SLL into durable remission, with no detectable disease and need for further treatment after completion of the fifteen-month trial.

Of course, these treatments weren't without their troublesome setbacks. One worrisome concern is that they would make me more immunocompromised. And this was particularly the case with obinutuzumab, which attacks the CD20 protein antigens. As Siddhartha Mukherjee writes in *The Song of the Cell* in discussing the development of antibodies against B cell lymphomas: "Attacking CD20-expressing lymphoma cells . . . inevitably precipitate a concomitant attack on B cells, rendering patients partly immune-compromised." It "wouldn't kill them," he notes, because new B cells are produced in the bone marrow.[17] But it would increase their vulnerability to infection and the seriousness of their illness for the time being, especially if they were already immunocompromised. This treatment-induced vulnerability was of considerable concern since I was immunocompromised and we were still in the pandemic.

Even still, given the potential success of the combined, experimental treatment—in addition to my wanting to start treatment—I thought joining the clinical trial was my best option. Several other factors also skewed my decision. One was that it was being offered at the nearby medical center with which I was associated as a client. Since clinical trials are most often conducted through medical training hospitals connected to large educational institutions, they can be quite distant for some prospective patients, thus requiring considerable travel or temporary relocation. Clearly that was not an issue in my case.

Another factor favoring the trial was financial. Cancer drugs are among the most expensive meds and continue to increase in cost, reportedly doubling "between 2009 to 2019, from an average monthly cost of $6,000 to nearly $15,000" without insurance. Even "Medicare beneficiaries without Medicare supplemental insurance" may "have out-of-the pocket expenses of $50,000 or more a year," and even patients with Medicare and good private insurance, such as myself, are likely to incur cancer drug costs in the vicinity of $10,000 a year.[18] There were other financial costs associated with the trial, but they were miniscule in comparison to the cost of the drugs. But the trial would cover the costs of the three clinical trial drugs, so there was a clear financial benefit to the trial, barring any unforeseen complications.

An additional reason I decided to participate (and a likely rationale for others) is that clinical trials are the principal pathway through which advances in cancer prevention, diagnoses, and treatments occur. Indeed, if not for clinical trials, it is likely that comparatively little would be known about cancer and its treatment. For example, if it weren't for clinical trials, none of the breakthrough targeted therapies that have become vetted treatment options for CLL/SLL over the past fifteen-plus years would be available. So however one's participation in a clinical trial might directly benefit themselves, it also provides an opportunity to contribute to a research enterprise that may increase scientific understanding of cancer and possibly help to make new or improved treatments available to those impacted by the targeted cancer or who will be victimized down the road. Basically, the trial is bigger than oneself. That alone struck me as a powerful incentive for participation.

As with all clinical trials, there are associated risks. There is the risk that the treatment regimen may have no effect and that the cancer may get worse during the trial. But that is also a possibility when one opts for the standard-of-care treatment. Equally concerning is that the study drugs can trigger various adverse side effects, some of which may be as deleterious as the cancer itself.

After I decided to participate, I read through the study's informed consent document, which details the study objectives, procedures, and risks, and which each trial participant must sign. I was struck by the daunting list of possible side effects associated with the three drugs. The probability of their occurrence ranged from common to occasional to rare, but with all possibly being serious. The most alarming to me were possible cardiovascular effects—particularly arrhythmia (atrial fibrillation) and even heart failure—associated principally with ibrutinib and secondarily with obinutuzumab. Also concerning was the possible occurrence of tumor lysis—when tumor cells are killed off by the treatment so quickly that the body can't adequately clear their contents from the bloodstream—and the prospect of it leading to renal failure requiring dialysis, which was the most worrisome side effect associated with venetoclax.

These concerning risks notwithstanding, the possibility of the clinical trial leading to remission and cessation of daily medication—as well as the financial and research factors—made my decision to go with the clinical trial option relatively easy. It was a no-brainer for Roberta and me. Moreover, since I would still be receiving the standard-of-care option whether I was randomly assigned to the control or experimental arm of the trial, I couldn't see any advantage in opting for the standard treatment alone.

That said, Roberta and I realized that my being enrolled in the clinical trial would involve substantially increasing treatment: more appointments with the oncology team, more blood draws, more radiology scans, taking more pills or other medications, and being monitored more closely in accord with the trial protocols. This entailed, as well, a long-term time commitment beyond the fifteen-month study treatment, with participants followed for ten years to monitor their condition, including oncology clinic visits every three months for six years and then every six months for the remaining four years. These might seem like weighty participant obligations, but not so much when one's well-being, and even life, is at stake. So, we did not construe these considerations as costs or burdens. Rather, we saw them as safeguards ensuring closer scrutiny of my overall condition as the trial progressed and beyond. Thus, what some trial candidates might see as disincentives for participation, we saw as additional incentives.

Given my declining condition, we were eager to begin treatment, so much so that the wait to begin on July 26 seemed interminable.

CHAPTER 6

Enduring the Clinical Trial and Its Iatrogenic Side Effects

Physicians at times inadvertently hurt their patients and occasionally they do so by the very devices they use in the effort to help them. There are diseases known as "iatrogenic." This complex-seeming term has enjoyed increasingly widespread use and merely means "of medical origin" or "arising from medicine."

—LOUIS SCHNEIDER[1]

Saturday before the trial began, one of the Friday night Zoom couples hosted a backyard barbeque gathering for the group. It was a revelatory gathering, since several of the participants, including Roberta and I, only knew each other virtually; it was the first time we'd met most of the others in person. Even more significantly, it was a touching gathering for me. Toward the end of dinner, the lead organizer of the group, a cardiologist, stood up, provided a few words of encouragement regarding the upcoming clinical trial, and handed me a wrapped gift he said might come in handy. It was a new best-selling novel: *While Justice Sleeps*, by the Georgia Democratic political organizer Stacey Abrams. I was happy to have the book because I had heard that it was a riveting legal-political thriller, but what was unexpectedly moving was when I opened it and saw that all of the participants had signed it with well wishes. Perhaps even more surprising was that what began as a temporary virtual Codenames gathering during the shelter-in-place phase of the pandemic had developed into a network of friends whose interactions now spilled into other corners of our lives. As Roberta and I drove home that evening, little did I know how handy that book would be as a time-filler in four days or so.

The trial began that following Monday on July 26. As a phase 3 trial, it was a large one with over four hundred patients, seventy-plus years of age, for whom this was their first treatment, enrolled at numerous sites across the US.[2] Half would be randomly assigned to the control arm of the study, with the other half to the experimental arm. Given the trial-based effectiveness of ibrutinib alone, or in combination with obinutuzumab, the odds were good that one would realize a progression-free outcome whatever arm they might be assigned. But Roberta and I were understandably interested in a remission outcome, just as we presume most enrollees were, so we were hopeful that I would be part of the experimental arm.

The stars were evidently aligned in our favor, as I was randomly assigned to the experimental group.

But before I began my first treatment, I received even more alarming evidence that my SLL was the likely cause of my night sweats and increasing fatigue earlier in the year. A bone marrow aspiration and biopsy I received that first day of the trial revealed trace evidence of the cancer in my blood stem cells. The percentage was relatively small, but it was sufficient in combination with the innumerable enlarged lymph nodes, low platelet count, and severe fatigue to designate the cancer as stage IV. Even though I was hobbled physically, I was still shocked when I was informed of this designation because of its frequent association with metastasis. The situation felt heavy, indeed. But my fears eased somewhat when I was assured that the staging criteria for all cancers aren't the same, and that metastasis wasn't a necessary condition for the stage IV designation in CLL/SLL. And now I would finally be receiving treatment.

Following a blood draw and appointment with the oncology nurse practitioner, I walked into the infusion lab on the second floor of the medical center cancer clinic for my initial treatment, which generated a sense of déjà vu. I had never been in this lab before, yet it was eerily familiar, no doubt because I had spent numerous hours in infusion labs like this one with my late wife, Judy. Although the locations, arrangement, and size of the labs were different, the ambience was strikingly similar. There were the infusion chairs that accommodated the patients, the IV poles standing like sentinels next to each chair and from which hung intravenous bags of saline solution and various chemo- and targeted therapies, the peripheral IV lines attached to the patients, and the adjacent chairs for an accompanying relative, friend, or caregiver. But what struck me most was the pervasive mood of solemnity. It was that mood, the gravity hanging in the air and the deference to the serious business at hand, that most gave me the sense I had been here before. But when I had been in spaces like this with Judy, I had been the caregiving spouse. Now, I was the patient.

These treatment contexts were also sometimes ambiguous and disorienting, which was especially the case during my first several days in the infusion center. I couldn't get ahold of what to make of it or how to feel about it. In my case, there was cognitive and emotional ambiguity, a sense of confusion. I didn't feel the anticipatory grief I did sitting beside Judy during her second episode of breast cancer with its metastasis and my feelings fluctuating between hope and despair, eventually drifting toward resignation. I didn't vacillate between one feeling or another, say between hope or hopelessness, because I didn't have a clear grasp of what was going on other than I was in an infusion lab initiating an expedition I never anticipated. In rummaging through the infusion memories, nothing functioned as an anchoring analogic frame that I could draw on to make sense of my experience. The fit wasn't right.

Complicating the situation was the lack of clarity about the exact character of the two control group drugs—ibrutinib pills and intravenous obinutuzumab—for which I was receiving my initial doses. Although the clinical trial "consent to participate" form I signed named the control and experimental drugs, it did not indicate whether they were chemotherapies or targeted therapies. The trial team told me that the drugs weren't chemotherapies, but when I sat in my infusion chair hooked up to the drip line, the hospital pharmacy delivered the vial of obinutuzumab in a container marked boldly with CHEMO on the side. Matching that label was the throwaway yellow paper gown and gloves the nurses all wore when attaching the vials of whatever drugs were being infused, presumably to provide protection from their toxicity. Confused, I thought maybe I was having chemotherapy dripped into me. Toward the end of the initial infusion, my experience was muddled further when a nurse handed me a plastic bag containing six or seven bottles of the ibrutinib pills and a piece of paper with CHEMO printed on it. On the way home that evening, I wondered aloud to Roberta if the two targeted drugs I began were also types of chemo. In the end, they weren't, but that wasn't clear to either of us at the time, given the chemo signage and the nurses' protective procedures.

Also making it difficult to get a hold on the experience was variation in the appearance of the patients. Some looked stereotypically frail and emaciated, as if they had been taking chemo for some time. Others appeared comparatively well, as if they were in recovery and looking nothing like the stereotypic cancer patient. I considered myself to be in this category: broad shouldered, now weighing around 190 pounds following the cancer-induced loss of thirty pounds, suntanned, and still with a head of receding hair. And still others looked like they were situated somewhere in between these two poles. I wondered, *What kinds of cancer did they have? What kinds of treatment were they receiving? And was there anything about their varied appearances that forecast what I might have in store?* But what I took away from the experience is that the physically observable manifestations of cancer can be quite varied. Nonetheless, a confluence of research indicates that the stereotypic, stigmatizing view still holds—even among some physicians treating cancer patients—no doubt amplifying most people's fear of cancer.[3]

These initial confounding experiences and observations in the infusion lab made it difficult to fit the first-day experience, as well as the subsequent infusions, into a coherent frame of what's going on. In a nutshell, I didn't have an unambiguous interpretive anchor or mooring.

Even so, the treatment schedule would continue with my taking the same dosage of ibrutinib pills daily for the duration of the trial, and the obinutuzumab infusion given two more times during the first twenty-eight-day cycle, followed by four more infusions given on the first day of cycles two through six. I wasn't scheduled to begin taking the pill-based venetoclax—the experimental drug—until early October, on the first day of cycle three, which I would continue daily through the course of the remainder of the trial. Like any schedule, it was just that—a schedule, a treatment plan. As with all such schedules, it was subject to modification with the occurrence of unanticipated contingencies.

Unanticipated contingencies and consequences are common occurrences on the heels of technological advances and even social and economic policy initiatives. A prime example is the evolving unanticipated effects of the widespread diffusion of the internet and various social media platforms, ranging from changes in dating and mating opportunities and patterns to changes in aspects of cognition and social connections, as with our shrinking attention span and the shallowness of our new "friended" social relationships. Sociologists have long referred to such phenomena as "unintended consequences." Economists have a similar concept called "externalities."

The medical lexicon has a parallel term that captures the unintended consequences of medical procedures or curatives that generate various noxious side effects, some of which may be more deleterious than the condition being treated. It is called iatrogenesis, with its effects dubbed iatrogenic. As with many concepts in medicine, and in science more generally, its roots can be traced back to Latin or classical Greek. Such is the case with iatrogenic, which is derived from Greek, with *iatros* meaning doctor or healer and *gennan* meaning "as a result." The word literally means "as a result of a doctor."[4] Broadly construed, then, iatrogenic means "of medical origin" or more crudely "killing by curing," but with the cautionary proviso that the adverse effects are unintentional.

Even though such adverse and undesirable effects of medical practice and treatment are unintentional, they are not uncommon. As Dr. Atul Gawande details in *Complications: A Surgeon's Notes on an Imperfect Science*, not only do medical mistakes happen, they are anything but aberrant. "The fact is" he writes, "that virtually everyone who cares for hospital patients will make serious mistakes, and even commit acts of negligence, every year."[5] But the scope of iatrogenic side effects is much broader than those induced by physician mistakes or oversights, as they also can be generated by all sorts of pharmaceutical treatments and interactions as well as the medical contexts in which the curative procedures and treatments take place. As a common folk saying warns, "If you want to get sick, go to the hospital."

I had been witness to such iatrogenic side effects before, with both Judy and later, Roberta. In the case of Judy, who passed away in the spring of 2005, she had a suspicious mammogram a year or so prior to having a mastectomy of her remaining breast due to a cancerous tumor. What made the mammogram suspicious is that it revealed a spot that the radiologist report dismissed as "a shadow." When the surgeon came out of the operating room to tell me and our daughters how the mastectomy went, she said that they were able to remove the breast without any other tissue damage, but they weren't able to get clear margins, meaning that cancerous tentacles now extended beyond the breast into the chest wall muscles. Once our daughters and I collected ourselves, my older daughter mentioned the earlier mammogram and the radiologist's reading of a suspicious spot as a shadow. The surgeon said without a hint of hesitation, "Now we know what that shadow was." If the radiologist did misread the original imagery, the consequences were dire for Judy, with the cancer eventually metastasizing to her brain and liver and leading to her passing two years later.

Turning to Roberta's experience with iatrogenic outcomes, she experienced a surgical oversight in the repair of an inguinal hernia. It was not as tragic as what happened to Judy, of course, but it came uncomfortably close to being so. Her initial surgery in August 2017 appeared to be routine, uneventful, and successful. However, toward the end of November she experienced increasing pain in her lower abdomen and groin, accompanied by nausea. She initially thought it was a severe urinary tract infection, but the medications she had previously taken for that had no curative effect, and her nausea, now accompanied by vomiting, had worsened. In the evening, we went to an urgent care but were sent home. The next day, with the symptoms even worse, we went to the nearby university walk-in and were immediately sent to the hospital emergency facility. A scan revealed a strangulated bowel due to a femoral hernia. Roberta was immediately prepped for surgery because of the various dangers associated with a strangulated bowel, such as perforation and systemic infection. The surgical team performed a bowel resection requiring a second abdominal incision, facilitating the surgical removal of the portion of the strangulated bowel and joining together the two healthy ends, followed by a week of hospital gastrointestinal treatment until her system sprang back to life. The oversight that led to this serious life-threatening situation was the failure to check to see if there was an emergent femoral hernia at the time of the inguinal hernia surgery, especially since femoral hernias are much more common in women than men, and particularly as women get older.[6] Although a different surgeon than one who did the inguinal surgery performed the emergency bowel resection, the first surgeon visited Roberta several times during her week in the hospital and openly apologized. The hospital chief of surgery, who also visited Roberta, further acknowledged and expressed his concern over the oversight, which he said would be presented in a surgical conference, presumably to educate the department and its trainees. Such can be the nature of iatrogenesis, but clearly with considerable variation in the consequences of its effects.

It is arguable that there are few, if any other, illnesses for which iatrogenic treatment effects are more common than for cancer. My sense is that most everyone who is being treated for some form of cancer via one or more chemotherapies or targeted therapies, or other pharmaceutical or radiological interventions, will incur one or more iatrogenic effects. That clearly appears to be the case for those enrolled in clinical trials, given that they are experiments with unpredictable side effects and outcomes for individual patients, the aggregate statistical side effects notwithstanding. Indeed, Dr. Siddhartha Mukherjee's bestselling book, *The Emperor of All Maladies: A Biography of Cancer,*[7] could just as appropriately be subtitled, *A Biography of Cancer Clinical*

Trails and Their Side Effects. Not only does Mukherjee feature clinical trials and their varied side effects throughout the book, but also he shows how comparatively little would be known about cancer in the absence of clinical trials. In the case of my clinical trial, I experienced a cascading flow of side effects—so many, in fact, that sometimes I felt like a walking textbook example of iatrogenesis.

After returning home following our first long, anxious ten-hour day at the infusion center, I got dressed for bed, looked in the bathroom mirror, and noticed that my abdomen—the primary site of my enlarged lymph nodes—wasn't as distended as the previous night. I yelled to Roberta, "The treatment already appears to be working. Is that possible?" Or was I experiencing an illusion based on wishful thinking? But it was no illusion. Roberta could see the shrinkage too. Clearly the treatments appeared to be working well, perhaps too well.

First thing the next morning I reported this sudden abdominal shrinkage to the trial team, with my oncologist arranging an appointment at a nearby, nonhospital infusion lab to get a saline drip to dilute the concentration of cancer metabolites in my system and wash them out. But a blood test showed that some of the kidney function markers were off, indicating my body was on the verge of tumor lysis. Tumor lysis references an emergency metabolic storm wherein large numbers of relatively new cancer cells that are growing uncontrollably are rapidly killed, generating a sizable number of metabolic toxins that must be flushed from the system. Since the kidneys remove most of such toxins, there is the danger of overwhelming the kidneys and the possibility of requiring dialysis. The usual precipitant of tumor lysis is some variant of chemotherapy or targeted tumor-reduction medication that does what it's supposed to do, albeit more effectively and quickly than intended.[8] In my case, the trigger was the interaction of the two control group drugs: ibrutinib and obinutuzumab.

My nurse practitioner called the oncologist, and they sent me to the hospital, with first a short stop at home to pick up a few things—my laptop and reading material, which included the gifted book from my Friday night Zoom-group friends. They were right that it would, indeed, come in handy.

I was hospitalized on the seventh floor in the oncology ward where my vital signs were taken and my blood drawn at frequent intervals. I received a constant drip of saline solution, coupled with a regimen of pills to normalize my phosphorous and uric acid levels and stymie the tumor lysis and threat to the kidneys. I didn't feel any pain, despite the threat of organ damage.

That night, I couldn't sleep or even drift off for any sustained time. Maybe it was my cocktail of medications or the difficulty getting comfortable in a hospital bed or simply anxiety from being hospitalized. Not even two melatonin were of much help. I believe I did doze off from two to three a.m. but was then awakened for a blood pressure check followed by a pee prompted by the saline solution being dripped into me, but after that I couldn't get back to sleep.

I stayed in the hospital for three days and nights. I spent much of the time reading the gifted book as well as talking with Roberta, my siblings and children, and a few friends who called. As I walked the halls while pulling or pushing my wheeled IV pole in search of ten thousand steps, I also chatted with the chief of hematology and his team when I encountered them. A month later, when I began taking venetoclax at the start of the experimental arm of the trial, I was again monitored for the possible reoccurrence of tumor lysis and, out of caution, hospitalized for a night. To my relief, it didn't materialize again, presumably because of the large number of cancer cells that had been killed during the first several days of the trial. While tumor lysis initially alarmed me, it turned out to be a side bar to the realization that the two control group drugs were working miraculously: reducing the size of my impacted lymph nodes in my abdomen and killing and flushing cancer cells from the system. The subsequent evolving side effects were much more troublesome, however, as they seemed to be interlaced in a cascading way with several enduring noxious outcomes.

From as early as the second week of the clinical trial, I experienced a second iatrogenic side effect. My platelet count was well below the lower normal threshold, typically lingering between 70,000 and 100,000 cells per microliter, resulting in quickened and excessive bruising. The normal range for these blood coagulants is 150,000–400,000. The major causal culprit was the ibrutinib pills, but it could have been the obinutuzumab infusion (and later venetoclax pills), since possible side effects for all three treatment drugs include bruising and bleeding. In any case, I didn't take the two control group drugs for a couple of weeks shortly after the trial began in order to push my platelet count upward. The low platelet count would remain an ongoing problem for the remainder of the trial and beyond, and even became worse when I was diagnosed with atrial fibrillation and required to take Eliquis (a blood thinner) about seven months down the road.

The third iatrogenic side effect was a profusion of skin issues. Sometimes it was just aggravating itchiness on the surface of the skin here and there; other times it was the appearance of what looked like isolated bug bites or hives; and for a while small, pinkish, fungal-looking patches developed in the lower abdominal area. I would usually send a picture of the affected area to my dermatologist, who would prescribe a remedial cream that would curtail the itching or eventually eliminate the aggravation. While the cause of the skin issues was not definitively diagnosable initially, in time it seemed quite likely that the issues were connected in part to the obinutuzumab infusion and the ibrutinib pills, both of which have skin issues listed as possible side effects.

But more troublesome than the itchy skin was its friability, that is, it became prone to tearing, fragmenting, and bleeding. In my case, the skin on the back of my hands and forearms seemed like a thin layer of paper, susceptible to being torn with the slightest abrasion. Of course, my increasing age and longtime exposure to the sun because of my lap swimming contributed to my skin's deteriorating condition, but the role of the clinical trial medications can't be discounted as causal agents. After all, I had been aging and engaging in sun-exposed lap swimming for some time, but it was only during the months of the clinical trial that my skin became so dangerously fragile.

One late autumn evening in 2021, Roberta and I left the infusion center where we had been since ten o'clock that morning. While waiting for an elevator, I coughed, and the strap of my laptop case slipped off my right shoulder. As the case fell to the floor, the edge of the strap deeply sliced the skin across my lower forearm. Laptop straps don't customarily function like knife blades, but this one did—it left a two-inch gash with flowing blood. I tried to staunch the bleeding with some Kleenex, but it was too profuse to stop with tissue or pressure. Fortunately, the door to the infusion ward had not locked, so we reentered and called upon the two remaining RNs to help us out. They quickly cleaned up the wound and closed it with steri-strips—thin adhesive bands that function much like regular stiches—across the gash to pull the skin together, and then wrapped the area with an elastic, tourniquet-like bandage. Roberta and I then made our second exit from the infusion center, and this time I held the handle of the laptop case rather than slinging the strap over my shoulder. As we thanked the RNs for their immediate combat-ready assistance, one of them said to me, "Be careful, your skin is very friable."

As with most accidents that occur in a flash, my impulse to take immediate ameliorative action—in this case to stop the bleeding— overwhelmed my initial feelings. So I was relieved when the two RNs did just that, but I was also somewhat shocked that it happened. And I was angry, not only at myself for bearing some responsibility but for having another issue to deal with. These were the times when I was most likely to feel down in the dumps, bordering on the edge of depression but without sinking into it or slumping into a bout of anomic confusion about the seriousness and life-defining salience of my condition. In those moments, I would find myself on the verge of surrendering to the identity of a cancer victim and the treatment process in which I was engulfed.

Such experiences and episodes heightened my consciousness of the fully and broadly embodied character of cancer. Whether it has colonized a single organ or the lymphatic or blood circulatory systems or crossed over metastatically to other organs and/or systems, it is broadly metastatic beyond the body in its reach into the networks and corners of the patient's life. Not only did my life change when I was diagnosed and subsequently joined the clinical trial, but Roberta's did too, as do the lives of every spouse or partner of a cancer victim as well as the lives of children and even extended family. In addition to the realignment of the daily routines of spouses and household members, extended family members' awareness of the relative's cancer etches it in their consciousness, as it now becomes a topic for discussion in subsequent encounters. Indeed, after my diagnoses and participation in the clinical trial, rarely did a phone conversation with one of my four siblings commence without a question about my condition and treatment. Such is the social-psychologically metastatic character of cancer, radiating beyond the victims into the lives and consciousness of their significant others.

Later that year, however, I would be engulfed by another series of Odyssey-like challenges that would push my SLL and clinical trial iatrogenic side effects from the front stage to the back stage of consciousness for nearly two months.

CHAPTER 7

A Forty-Five-Day COVID Intrusion

Through the summer and fall of 2021, the Delta variant of COVID had been the major strain, but as the year faded into winter, its dominance was supplanted by the Omicron strain. In late November, the World Health Organization initially recognized Omicron as a "variant of concern" because of its ease of transferability. Indeed, after its detection in South Africa and Hong Kong, it spread across the globe like a wind-aided wildfire. On December 1 the California and San Francisco Departments of Public Health identified its initial US case, and by the week ending on Christmas Day, the CDC estimated that Omicron now accounted for 77 percent of all COVID cases in the country.[1]

Not a good time for relaxed holiday gatherings. But just as most citizens the world over were caught unawares by the initial coronavirus variant in late February 2020, they were insufficiently attentive or indifferent to the Omicron variant and the ease and speed of its spread. Our family was among these vulnerable citizens, even though we thought we were appropriately cautious.

Roberta and I climbed out of bed at around seven on Christmas day to get ready to drive thirty minutes south to our daughter's home to open gifts with our older children and grandchildren and spend the remainder of the day together. The six adults were all vaccinated twice, the two kids once, and four of us had received the first booster shot. Being immunocompromised, I wore a mask much of the day, as did Roberta, except when eating or having something to drink. The gathering expanded when several of my daughter's friends came by in the late afternoon and early evening. As far as we knew, all guests were vaccinated at least once. The only certain exceptions were two young neighbor kids, who came walking through the living room a number of times in the early evening. With most everyone circling around the island counter in the middle of the kitchen, Roberta and I kept our distance in the living room. On our way home that evening we reflected on the lovely Christmas Day, but wondered whether anyone at the gathering was carrying the rapidly spreading Omicron variant and whether we had been sufficiently cautious.

The following two days were uneventful. Roberta and I relaxed as we customarily did the few days after Christmas, swimming our laps on Sunday and walking on Monday. We retired on Monday night feeling no worse for the wear, but that feeling of relative well-being dissipated overnight. I awakened Tuesday morning with a cough, some chest congestion, body aches, and feeling warm and fatigued. Roberta took my temperature, and the thermometer read 101, so Roberta and I anxiously took the home COVID antigen test. While my various symptoms were telltale physical manifestations of the Omicron variant, I wistfully hoped they might be symptomatic of the onset of a nasty cold. No such luck, however. Even though Roberta's test was negative, mine was boldly positive. Hoping it was a mistake, I took another test an hour later.

The result was the same: I had COVID.

I was upset and frustrated. Roberta and I thought we had been doing all the right things to reduce the probability of catching the virus. Clearly, though, it appears that we weren't sufficiently vigilant at my daughter's Christmas Day gathering, as one or more people were shedding the virus. And I wasn't the only one—my two daughters and a son-in-law fell ill a few days later.

Roberta and I immediately started taking additional precautions. That night we began sleeping in different bedrooms, we wore masks whenever together in the same room, and we were conscientious hand washers. Roberta continued to be symptom-free and test negative perhaps because of these measures; good luck or some internal resistance to COVID may have also benefitted Roberta, as she had experienced the same exposure as I did on Christmas Day, and she had been sleeping next to me when I awakened with COVID a few days later. Whatever the reasons she was able to ward it off, not being infected allowed her to continue in the caregiver role she had assumed well before I began the clinical trial.

My catching COVID was particularly worrisome for Roberta and me. Not only was I immunocompromised because of the SLL, but the obinutuzumab monoclonal antibody that I had been taking rendered me even more vulnerable. As I noted earlier, obinutuzumab targets both cancerous and normal B cells—which generate antibodies that identify and attack pathogens—meaning the healthy B cells are also neutralized, thus decreasing one's immunity and resistance to infection.

Adding another layer of concern was the risk of severe COVID complications, hospitalization, and even death, with the prospect increasing with age as well as with certain medical conditions and dis-abilities. Early studies of COVID-19 mortality rates in the spring of 2020 into the spring of 2022 found that persons sixty-five and older accounted for around 80 percent of all COVID deaths in the US, and this was especially the case for those with co-morbidities. One study of mortality risk among patients hospitalized for COVID during the Delta and Omicron variant periods reported, "The majority of in-hospital deaths occurred among adults aged ≥65 years (81.9%) and persons with three or more underlying medical conditions (73.4%)."[2] Even though I had only one serious underlying medical condition at the time—the SLL—I was in the vulnerable age category.

It was with these concerns in mind that I texted my clinical trial coordinator the morning I tested positive. Having been in the clinical trial for five months, I had learned that one of its advantages is that you have ready access to your trial team by contacting the trial coordinator. I informed her that I had just tested positive and was experiencing a number of the telling symptoms. Within hours, the clinical trial coordinator told me that my oncologist had ordered and scheduled a PCR test for me the next day. The drive-through PCR test—arranged without getting out of the car in a parking lot near the medical center—confirmed the positive home antigen test results, as if I needed additional confirmation given the robustness of my symptoms.[3]

Shortly after the positive PCR, my oncologist prescribed sotrovimab, a new monoclonal antibody treatment for COVID. The previously used monoclonal antibody treatment, REGEN-COV, which had been effective in mitigating the Delta strain, was ineffective against Omicron. And even though sotrovimab had just received FDA approval, it wasn't yet widely available. Fortunately, the medical center at which I was a patient was one of the few hospitals in the county and beyond to have secured a supply of sotrovimab. I was scheduled for an IV infusion on December 30, two days after the onset of the flurry of symptoms.

On a dismal overcast and drizzling morning, Roberta and I drove to the medical center for my appointment. Making it even more gloomy was the dearth of activity at the usually bustling medical center. It was like a ghost town. Few cars in the parking lots. No one walking here or there. Being the week after Christmas accounted in part for the vacant ambience, but the grip of Omicron was an even more pressing reason.

Roberta dropped me off, and I quickly found the locked door to the secluded infusion room on the first floor of a building at least a hundred yards from the main hospital buildings and ER. The hospital kept the room's location and access instructions confidential except to those affected patients who had received a physician's prescription because of their vulnerability to severe COVID illness and hospitalization. With an outdoor entrance, COVID patients like myself wouldn't need to walk through an indoor corridor to access the makeshift infusion room. Indeed, I was still fully symptomatic; I still had a low-grade fever (fluctuating with Tylenol), body aches, cough, congestion, runny nose, and fatigue. In addition, in the midst of Omicron's spread reaching epidemic proportions, with the demand for mitigating treatments exceeding the supply by a long shot, the hospital was concerned about people walking in who were neither infected nor immunocompromised.

To gain entrance, I texted my name, identifying information, and appointment time to the hospital staff inside. I waited a few minutes for an infusion chair to be vacated, and within a few minutes, the door clicked open. I was ushered into what looked like a large, converted storage room that was quite barren except for the twelve to fifteen infusion chairs arranged about eight feet apart in a semicircle. An assortment of fully masked individuals occupied the chairs, all hooked up to their own IV drip line. Demographically, the patients appeared to be mostly sixty-plus years old, predominantly White but of varied nationality. Most of them were local, aside from a traveling resident of Tennessee who was scheduled to return home until he came down with COVID and received a physician's recommendation for sotrovimab, presumably because of his vulnerabilities.

A nurse wearing a throwaway paper protective gown over her uniform, as well as a mask and a plastic face shield, led me to the vacant chair.

I just sat, asking no questions but listening to whatever I could pick up—eavesdropping again. The conversation was sparse and concentrated among three men in one corner of the room and an older Iranian couple across from me, but based on what little I heard, the facial expressions of the patients, and the posture, comments, and protective gear of the three attending nurses, the ambience was a contradictory mixture of relief and uncertainty. Relief that a mitigating antidote was being administered but anxiety about the severity of the COVID cases and the treatment's effectiveness. The gloomy weather, coupled with the guarded seclusion of and access to the makeshift lab, peppered the whole experience with a dose of darkness.

That melancholy aside, I left an hour or so after the vial of sotrovimab was emptied with hope it would mute my COVID symptoms and keep me out of the hospital. Sure enough, in less than twenty-four hours it was proving to be a magic potion. My fever abated and my body aches dissipated. I still had a cough, a runny nose, fluctuating fatigue, but little aggravating chest congestion. I didn't feel great, but I felt better than the previous two days, and my concern about being hospitalized had diminished.

Even as I began a new phase of my cancer odyssey—being ill with and being treated for COVID—I found that there were several advantages to the clinical trial that facilitated the attention and support I received not only for my cancer treatment, but also especially during my bout with COVID. One was the accessibility and responsiveness of the trial team. Access to timely and quality health care is a perennial issue, especially with disparities by race, ethnicity, social class, geographic location, and insurance status.[4] But clinical trials can mute some of these complicating factors. And mine did, as accessibility was never an issue. The trial team was always within reach, whether by text or cell; I had the cell number of my oncologist and my clinical trial coordinator. They told me to text or call whenever I felt it was necessary, typically beginning with the coordinator. Whenever I had a concern, I would thus text the trial coordinator with little hesitancy. She would immediately pass on the message to my oncologist or NP, who would respond directly or through the coordinator with little, if any, delay.

While I was actively sick with COVID, I was told to keep the clinical trial coordinator informed regarding my condition and ongoing test results. I would send her text messages after each positive test, and shortly after she would pass on the oncologist's decision to cancel an upcoming obinutuzumab infusion because of its dilution of whatever compromised immune capacity I had for fighting off the COVID virus. Or she might instruct me to suspend the ibrutinib for a week or two, waiting until the virus died off and I tested negative. My oncologist focused on managing the risk of the virus versus the cancer, deciding to postpone my cancer treatments for two weeks.

At this time, Roberta's role as caretaker became even more challenging because I was mostly confined to the house until I tested negative and wasn't carrying and shedding the virus. So errands and chores that I had been handling, or that we had been doing together, now fell into Roberta's lap. The week I tested positive, for example, she ran to the nearby CVS pharmacy, did the grocery shopping, and did most of the daily household chores. Eight days after I tested positive, I was scheduled to drive to the medical center to pick up a new batch of my targeted therapy pills, but I was still symptomatic and positive, so going to the hospital wasn't a smart idea. Roberta went on her own, negotiating the crowded afternoon freeways to make the twenty-five-mile round trip to pick up my pills. At this time, I hadn't been out of the house since the Monday after Christmas other than to get the PCR test and the sotrovimab infusion.

By the first few days of January 2022, it was clear that I wasn't alone in catching COVID; Omicron's rapid spread had pushed the daily count of new infections to around a million, which was the highest of any country in the world. Toward the end of the month the CDC reported that it accounted for 99 percent of all current cases in the US. Clearly it was spreading at lightning-like speed. If there was any consolation to the new variant's dominance and virulent diffusion, it was that it appeared to trigger milder symptoms than the previous strains. Still, just as the number of Omicron cases were rising on the cusp of the new year, so were the number of hospitalized COVID patients, with a 50 percent increase in the first week of January.[5]

One full week after initially testing positive for COVID, on an early afternoon on a beautiful, blue-skied day with only a few puffs of visible white clouds, I sat in the living room thinking gloomily about my situation. I looked across the bay with the river of water below to the bluff with rows of tiered housing. Particularly noticeable were the tall palm trees, standing like toothpick sentinels overlooking the bay. The sunlight bent its way around the east side of the house and into the windowed living room, bouncing off the couch and warming the entire room. Several hawks flew above, barely flapping their large wings as they caught the air currents and floated precariously close to the windows. A truly picturesque setting.

And yet, there I sat feeling down and sorry for myself. And for good reason. Not only had I contracted COVID a week earlier, but it was on top of bladder cancer, SLL, skin cancers, weeks of radiation, the clinical trial including seven chemo pills a day, and an unpleasant-looking skin rash. "That's a lot of shit to deal with over the past several years," I mumbled to myself, "and a lot of heavy-duty fuel to fire some level of depression."

Having COVID on top of the cancer and clinical trial provided ample reason for feeling down, but what I found most frustrating was feeling so helpless and constrained. Other than going for walks in the open air, which Roberta and I tried to do several times a day, I rarely went out. I didn't even go swimming—which had become a ritualized activity three times a week for the past forty-five years—out of concern of spreading the virus. Even if the odds were low of actually infecting swimmers in adjacent lanes in an outdoor pool, would they really be comfortable knowing that the person free-styling next to them was symptomatic with COVID? How would or should I respond when someone asked, "How are you doing?" Tough to say "great," especially when I had come to know more about most of them beyond their being just fellow swimmers. That I had the energy to walk and think about swimming at that point clearly indicated that I was feeling better. I was still symptomatic with a runny nose and a slight cough, but they were nagging annoyances rather than immobilizing ailments.

Being more of an optimist inclined to look for the light rather than the darkness, serious depression was not in accord with my psychic disposition. No doubt I felt down now given the confluence of COVID with all my other medical issues, but sinking into ongoing depression was not in the cards. Depression antidotes—such as the beautiful view from my living room—were certainly in play whenever I brooded about the accumulating and intersecting ailments and side effects. And probably most important of all to preventing a further downward slide were the intersecting networks of support with Roberta at the hub, which I speak more about in chapter 12.

In mid-January, three full weeks after testing positive, I woke up feeling invigorated with plans to lap swim for the first time since the day after Christmas and then drive up the 405 freeway to see my son, daughter-in-law, and granddaughter, and one of my daughters and grandson. I hadn't tested since the previous Thursday, which revealed a faint positive line, so I thought perhaps there would be no such faint line today. But no such luck—I tested positive once again. And today's test showed even a stronger, sharper positive line. How depressing! I called my son to let him know it was best to cancel today's plans and not run the risk of exposing my granddaughter. I then talked to my daughter, who reminded me that canceled plans seemed to be one of the common trappings of the spread of Omicron.

Equally frustrating as the social engagement disruptions and postponements were the underlying fluctuations in the severity of the symptoms. One morning I might awaken feeling energized and pretty much symptom-free, as just noted, and a day or so later the previously noxious symptoms might resurface with renewed potency. But it wasn't lingering symptoms or the virus's two-week derailing of the trial treatment regimen that made the ordeal so aggravating and tiresome. Most frustrating was its constraining curtailment of my everyday life. It was like being pushed back into the earlier lockdown mode, with few outings beyond the confines of the house other than for medical appointments and walking outside.

As I coped with the restlessness and fatigue of my ongoing infection, my dreams indicating the loss of my geographic compass returned. More surprising, however, were the recent dreams of troublesome loss associated with my late and current wives. In one, Judy was pursuing a divorce. But shortly after each dream, I would awaken in the twilight zone with a feeling of puzzlement—she and I had never discussed separating—and then relief, knowing that dreamt divorce wasn't possible since she was deceased. The other dream involved a similar loss of my current wife, Roberta. I feared, but couldn't substantiate, that she may have been meeting other men for lunch. As with the other dream, the fear of spousal loss was quickly muted when I awakened to her by my side with immediate recollection of her attentive caregiving throughout my illness odyssey. That both were attractive women—Judy, with her strawberry blonde hair and feisty but engaging personality, and Roberta, a model-like five foot ten with shoulder-length silver hair with strands of original blonde and an appealing personality—perhaps added to my insecurity? But who knows for certain? As neuroscientist and brain surgeon Rahul Jandial writes in his analysis of why we dream, "There is no way to objectively prove if a dream," or its causes, have "been interpreted correctly."[6] But given the daily dose of fourteen pills, half of which were trial targeted therapy pills, along with the intersection of the SLL, COVID, and the clinical trial and its treatment complications, it is probably of little surprise that my mind would spawn dreams of vulnerability and loss. Indeed, my journey was most trying during the overlap of the clinical trial and my long bout with COVID, when I was most compromised physically and psychologically, thus increasing my vulnerability to such threatening dream-state losses.

A month after testing positive, I awakened feeling more fatigued than before I went to bed, along with a stuffy nose and congested head. Not surprisingly, I tested positive as well, and so informed my oncologist. She responded with directions to suspend both sets of targeted therapy pills (the ibrutinib and venetoclax) and cancel the obinutuzumab infusion scheduled for later in the week because of their probable suppression of whatever little immunity I might still have to fight off the COVID. However, I did retain my late-week appointment with the oncology nurse practitioner—in person but with masks on—who indicated that I should continue to hold off taking the seven daily targeted therapy pills until my COVID abated. This could still be for a while, she added, since there is some evidence that COVID seems to linger for immuno-compromised CLL patients. She gave two examples: one patient who tested positive for ninety days and another for fifty days. Today marked thirty-two days, so clearly it was lingering for me as well. And consistent with the haphazard fluctuation in the severity of my symptoms, today I felt better than I had in the past three days.

But the waning symptoms reversed course as Friday slithered into the weekend, with a wearisome fatigue seeping in late afternoon and intensifying into the evening and Saturday morning, driving me onto the couch for most of the day with disinterest in doing much of anything other than watching two NFL playoff games. I hadn't experienced such immobilizing tiredness since the first couple days of being afflicted, so I felt frustrated and discouraged with what I felt might be a relapse and indication of a slide into long COVID, which the NP remarked was "of concern."

The following Thursday, still testing positive but feeling much better, I had another appointment with the oncologist. The main takeaway was that she was still carefully weighing the tricky balance between decreasing COVID symptoms and possibly increasing the SLL symptoms in order to decide when to resume treatment. "We'll go another week," she said, "and review next Thursday after blood tests, careful review of symptoms, and an exam of my spleen and lymph nodes." She stressed that the trial team wanted to monitor me carefully with respect to restarting the treatment because it might cause my COVID symptoms to increase again and possibly throw me into long COVID.

At this point my symptoms were mild (intermittent tiredness, getting chilled easily, and some nasal congestion) and were declining in their severity, which was, as my oncologist emphasized, "a hopeful sign." We discussed being around family, and she felt it was safe to be around vaccinated people with no symptoms. Feeling somewhat better but frustrated with being shut in for almost a month, emboldened, I asked, "What about a Super Bowl Sunday gathering?"

"Let's not get that far out yet," she responded cheerfully. "Next Thursday could look a lot different."

Five days later, on Tuesday, February 8, my condition did begin to look a lot different. I tested positive again in the morning, but with the faintest line to date. I understood that "a positive is a positive, no matter how faint the line," but a fainter line might indicate "less virus in the body" and "that a person is less sick, less infectious, or further along in their infection."[7] That's how I read the faint line. Having been infected with the virus now for forty-three days, I may have been engaged in wishful thinking or self-deception. But I thought otherwise since my symptoms had been fading as well. Both the nasal congestion and fatigue had mostly vanished. I also took the dog for a brisk mile and a half walk in the morning without any discomfort or fatigue, so things appeared to be moving in the right direction. I texted the oncology team that I tested positive again but indicated that I was feeling quite good.

I was also upbeat about my scheduled Evusheld shots in the afternoon. Evusheld was a new monoclonal antibody that was supposed to help guard against COVID infection by boosting the antibodies of patients who are immunocompromised and don't gain much protection from vaccination. However, my spirit was dampened shortly after arriving for my appointment when I was told it had been canceled because I was still testing positive and the off-site clinic didn't have an extra room to isolate me from the other patients. So I was rescheduled for the next Tuesday, contingent, of course, on testing negative, which I believed would be the case given this morning's faint line and the waning symptoms.

Two days later, after taking our dog for a morning walk, I took the home test in hopes that the faint line of two days ago would be non-existent today. And it was! At least that's how it appeared to me when I first looked at the register. No second line. The faint line of two days ago had now vanished. But not fully believing what I saw, I kept check-ing it repeatedly while I was doing my dumbbell weight-lifting routine. I returned for another look after completing each set, thinking that maybe I'd seen a mirage triggered by wishful thinking. After all, it had now been forty-five days since I initially tested positive. So as soon as Roberta returned home from swimming, I showed her the register, and she validated what I thought I saw initially—a negative test—which ushered in a wave of relief.

After embracing with a newfound joy, I contacted the clinical trial coordinator to pass on the long-awaited good news and to see if Thursday's appointment should be canceled in favor of the rescheduled appointment for the Evusheld shots. I heard back shortly to proceed with the Evusheld treatment with the hope that the injected antibodies would reduce my vulnerability to catching the virus again. Even though my Evusheld appointment had been postponed a week, the coordinator assured me it would still be available. I asked because I had read that this new antiviral medication was in short supply, just as the sotrovimab had been in December.

The demand for both monoclonal antibodies exceeded their supply by a sizeable margin. A *Los Angeles Times* story had just reported that fewer than six hundred thousand doses of Evusheld had been sent to medical facilities country-wide for vulnerable patients, which is only a drop in the bucket of the estimated seven-million-plus immunocompromised adults in the US.[8] I learned from the oncology team that the medical center had been aggressive in combatting COVID from its inception, which might have explained why the hospital was an initial recipient of sotrovimab and Evusheld, along with Paxlovid for newly detected COVID victims. This, along with being close to a medical center with oncologists specializing in the study and treatment of specific cancers, including CLL/SLL, and having access to a clinical trial without having to travel far, accented the good fortune of my living in an area in which there are a number of accessible, high-quality medical facilities. As my oncologist reminded me, getting the sotrovimab within two days of coming down with the Omicron variant not only reduced the severity of my symptoms, but may very well have kept me out of the hospital.

The sense of relief that came with knowing that I had now escaped the grip of COVID, with its hold on me for a month and a half, was understandably palpable. Not only for Roberta and me, but for my entire family. But that sense was muffled by the even more pressing battle I was waging against the SLL variant of lymphoma and the fifteen-month clinical trial of which I was only halfway through. The next day, after testing negative, I was back on track resuming the daily regimen of ibrutinib and venetoclax pills and rescheduling the postponed obinutuzumab infusion. Little did we know that in less than two weeks I would begin to encounter another set of challenges triggered by a new series of cascading treatment side effects. Much like Odysseus's journey, my odyssey was encumbered by one obstacle after another.

CHAPTER 8

Cascading Iatrogenesis: Heart Problems and Declining Vision

In late February 2022, two weeks after I finally tested negative for COVID, I was scheduled for my sixth and final infusion of obinutuzumab, which had been on hold because of my COVID. But the preceding Saturday, I had an irregular heartbeat and lightheadedness, and the oncology nurse practitioner scheduled an electrocardiogram (EKG) before my infusion. I may have had symptoms prior to Saturday morning, February 19, but I didn't feel any telltale indicators until that morning. In fact, an echocardiogram I had earlier that month showed no signs of any irregularity with my heart or heartbeat.

The EKG results indicated atrial fibrillation (AFib), an irregular and often rapid heart rhythm that can lead to stroke, heart failure, and other complications,[1] which constituted my fourth and most serious iatrogenic side effect to date. So the infusion was postponed, and I was scheduled for a cardiology consult later that afternoon. As I sat in the clinic office waiting to see the scheduled cardiology nurse, my anxiety was intense, not only because of the new malady, but also because it was one more medical condition to deal with. Not surprisingly, it manifested when my blood pressure was taken, which was much higher than normal, and I was prescribed Eliquis, a now popular blood thinner, and metoprolol, which can slow the heart rate.

After picking up the drugs and returning home that evening—some ten hours after arriving at the infusion lab in the morning—I thought back to a few days before my EKG; perhaps I had been experiencing symptoms of AFib but hadn't paid enough attention. Just before taking our dog for a morning walk, I took my first prescribed vitamin D3 50,000-unit capsule due to low vitamin D and presumably because of reports of higher levels being beneficial for some types of cancer, including lymphoma.[2] As we began to ascend a short hill about a third of a mile into the walk, I felt a wave of tiredness wash over me along with lightheadedness. I continued the walk for around a half mile, stopping once to bend over and tie my shoe, after which I felt very lightheaded again. I returned home, sat down for a bit, and talked with one of my daughters about the best time to visit on Sunday. As soon as I got up I felt faint. I grabbed the counter and put my head down for a minute to regain my equilibrium and then lay down and took my blood pressure twice, with relatively normal readings that hovered around 125/78. I remained intermittently lightheaded throughout the day, particularly after getting up from sitting. After reading about possible side effects of the high-dose vitamin D3 capsule I had taken, I thought the lightheadedness was perhaps due to a rush of vitamin D toxicity.

It's possible that the supplement, despite its suggested benefits for certain cancers, may have contributed to my heart problems; some research has indicated that "too much vitamin D can lead to the onset of atrial fibrillation."[3] The verdict is inconclusive, however, with a Mayo

Clinic summary report on vitamin D indicating a high dose "might cause" heart rhythm issues.[4] But so can the clinical trial drugs, particularly ibrutinib. Ibrutinib in combination with obinutuzumab appear to have been the major precipitants; the clinical trial consent form listed "abnormal heartbeat which may cause fainting" and possibly "other heart issues" as side effects for both. Whether the emergent arrhythmia was due to the trial medications or the large dose of vitamin D, or the interaction of the two, is difficult to determine with certainty. What was not debatable, however, is the fact that I now had a newly diagnosed cardiac problem to go along with the cancer.

The evening after the EKG, I felt depressed again. *Can't seem to get a medical break*, I thought, *with one damn new medical issue piling on top of another*. But sensing that I was on the verge of sinking into a gloomy dark hole, I caught myself. "What good does it do to feel sorry for myself?" I asked. Self-pity certainly doesn't facilitate the healing process. Moreover, being more inclined to see "the glass half full than half empty," I reminded myself that neither the lymphoma nor the electrical heart malfunction is a death sentence, at least not in the short run. Besides, I was still able to walk and lap swim, and stay reasonably connected with immediate family and friends, both of which are nonmedicative antidotes to depression. "But damn," I mused aloud, "why do I have to deal with a number of ailments at once, including constantly monitoring my previously diagnosed but under control bladder cancer, for which I have a cystoscopy next Friday?" But then, to defuse that question and perhaps normalize my situation, I told Roberta, "You know, I guess I'm finally coming to the realization that being in our seventies does push us toward that nebulous age category called the elderly. And these various medical conditions do cluster among folks in that category, right?"

So yes, I felt down in the dumps and even sorry for myself from time to time, but these bouts of gloom usually passed in relatively short order rather than persisting, as with immobilizing depression, because of the intersection of the various depression antidotes—my "glass half full" disposition, the context in which I lived, recognition that many others have a more troublesome set of issues than mine, the age-related normalization of my overlapping conditions, and a web of supportive allies including Roberta (of course) and my family and friends, and the number of medical professionals I could turn to for their expertise and guidance.

As I grappled with yet another diagnosis and medical complication, my previously discussed low platelet count remained a pressing issue. But it dropped even lower and became more erratic shortly after I began taking the prescribed recommended dosage of Eliquis. As an anticoagulant used to prevent and treat blood clots, it is likely that Eliquis increased my vulnerability to bleeding and bruising. But it wasn't the only culprit, as I had been still taking the ibrutinib pills, as well as the obinutuzumab infusion and venetoclax pills, for which easy bruising and bleeding are noted as possible side effects. Whatever the exact role these drugs played in depressing my platelet count and increasing the time it took for my blood to clot beyond normal, the easy bleeding during a blood draw or a slight abrasion or bump and the seemingly perpetual dark-blue bruises on my forearms and the back of my hands offered ongoing evidence that the medications were complicit coconspirators.

With the occurrence of these and more serious treatment hitches down the trial road, I was reminded again that this odyssey-like journey is not linear, but is characterized by steps forward and back, and then sideways and, hopefully, forward again. Rather than a clearly mapped trajectory, the journey has a haphazard, helter-skelter character to it.

But it wasn't the AFib and the low platelet count that were the worst of these iatrogenic side effects. A new unsettling occurrence would throw me into the next and most trying stage of my cancer odyssey.

On the morning of April 28, I noticed an abnormality in the vision of my left eye when I woke up and couldn't read my cell phone without reading glasses. I'd never needed them previously, as several years earlier I'd had cataract surgery that set the lens in my left eye for reading short and intermediate distances. But now I couldn't read anything through the left eye. All I could see was a dark oblong block, like a large but stable floater, skewed toward the nasal side of my eye. It reminded me of a solar eclipse when the moon passes between the sun and the earth. Whatever the best descriptive analogy, the result was that my left eye was of limited use. It wasn't technically blind yet, as I did have some peripheral vision and could see light and vague images, but nothing was clear. Not much of a consolation, though, since I couldn't read, look at the computer screen, or even worse, see and discern the faces of those with whom I was interacting. Thankfully, I could do all of that with my right eye, with the assistance of readers for reading and working at the computer.

The retinal ophthalmologist who took the lead indicated that the problem was a retinal bleed, and that while my incipient macular degeneration may have made my eye more vulnerable to a retinal hemorrhage, my persistent low platelet count had triggered the condition. My oncologist had been concerned about my platelet count, and even suspended the ibrutinib for a time, which increased the count, but it still remained well below the normal lower threshold of 150; it had dropped to just 35 not more than three weeks earlier. It had bounced upward with some modification of the trial drug regimen, but it was still well below 100. In other words, had it not been for the low platelet count, the probability of the hemorrhage would have been reduced considerably.

Upon initial examination, the retinal specialist emphasized, "This is a very serious condition that we might be able to slow down with proper treatment."

"Perhaps one or all of the trial drugs should be stopped?" I asked.

"No," he said. "The lymphoma is the more serious of the two conditions," he emphasized, "and that even with this consequence it should not be stopped."

During that appointment, as well as for the next two, I received eye injections to stop the bleeding, but they weren't very effective.

In spite of that, for the next several months, I continued with my daily routines and various commitments the best I could for someone not only in the midst of a clinical trial but also confronted with the concerning loss of vision in one eye. And I continued to negotiate interactions with colleagues or friends, doubting how much most others really needed to know about my condition, ailments, or overall journey. I was hesitant about conveying much information. Additionally, the interactional context of most encounters often didn't spare much time for an elaborated response. Both considerations were at play when I attended a late afternoon retirement gathering for a colleague in early June, as was my ongoing confusion about the salience of my cancer as an identity peg. As I walked up to the entrance, two colleagues standing outside, and whom I hadn't seen for some time, said, "You look great and really fit." And another said shortly, after I was inside and about to take a seat, "You look slim and good. Is that what retirement does for you?" My instantaneous thought in both encounters was a quizzical one: *Do I just acknowledge such comments and questions, say thanks, and move on? Do I direct attention away from me to them by asking, "How are things going?" Or do I treat the comments and questions as an occasion to respond to their queries?*

In the case of the first encounter, since we were just a few steps from entering the room where the event was being held, I limited my response to "Thanks" and "Good to see you." In the latter instance, wherein we had a few minutes before the event was called to order, I provided an abbreviated answer, saying, in so many words, "No, it's not retirement. I've just been trying to stay fit while being in a clinical trial for a type of lymphoma."

"I'm sorry to hear that," my colleague said, "but you look like you're doing okay."

"Thanks," I responded. "I am doing well, all things considered." The first response was a courteous deflection, and the second one was a constrained response, with neither conveying much about my odyssey.

Their consensual response that I "looked good" suggested that their comparative reference was probably the stereotypical cancer patient who looked frail and unsteady, balding, pale with sunken eyes, and often wearing a headscarf if a woman—a perception that had applied to Judy but not to me. As my oncologist told me during an early summer appointment in 2022, "Well, you look good, and you don't look like many cancer patients," my complaints about the fourteen pills I took each day and their side effects notwithstanding.

However I appeared to others, it masked the two most troublesome side effects: the AFib and the waning vision of my left eye. With the hope of kicking my heart back into normal sinus rhythm, my cardiologist performed a cardioversion with transesophageal echocardiogram at the end of June. Roberta and I left the hospital optimistically with my heart in normal rhythm after the procedure, but our hopes of its durability were dashed in a day and a half when it fell back into AFib.

The condition of my left eye wasn't improving either. At the next appointment with my retinal ophthalmologist in mid-August, tests revealed that there had been no discernible changes in the vision in my left eye and that the injections weren't affecting the hemorrhage, so the injections were suspended. He mentioned surgery as a possibility, but with reluctance because of my still low platelet count. He was also doubtful that the surgery would make any difference because of probable optic nerve damage and other factors. He consulted with other retinal experts, and they concurred. The verdict was straightforward: The impaired vision in my left eye was now chronic and probably immutable.

This was another one of those moments when fear escalated to the surface of my consciousness and autocratically consumed my thoughts. In this case, it was the fear of impending blindness in my left eye. And if that weren't concerning enough, I received a call around that time from my urologist's office telling me that the lab results of my urine specimen from the recent cystoscopy contained some suspicious cells, and he wanted me to get a FISH urine test. FISH (fluorescence in situ hybridization) analysis is an FDA-approved, urine-based marker that "maps" the genetic material in human cells and assists in diagnosis and surveillance of invasive urothelial cancer. The call was somewhat of a shock, since my last cystoscopy showed a clean, healthy-looking bladder, and my recent appointment with my oncologist was all upbeat. The call was like another dark cloud appearing suddenly out of nowhere, bringing with it a feeling of melancholy and uncertainty as to what this might mean. Here we go again, I feared. One mounting challenge after another. Just as some undiagnosed corporal agitation is likely to trigger thoughts of an emergent cancer or metastasis, so are messages, especially unanticipated ones, from a physician recommending a new test. After getting the test the following week, I anxiously awaited the results, an experience I have repeated time and again, as have all people with cancer when awaiting the results of a recent CT scan, MRI, bone marrow biopsy, blood test, or urine specimen.

Judy and I experienced similar anxieties while awaiting the results of her scans for breast cancer over the course of seventeen years between the spring of 1988 when she was first diagnosed and her passing in the spring of 2005. And now, for the past several years, I have found myself, along with Roberta, experiencing those same anxieties. Fortunately, they are not enduring, with good reports and the demands of living often muting their clamor, but even then, they linger at the edge of my conscious awareness, ready to be activated with calls like I received that August afternoon.

Relevant to such occurrences, a fellow sociologist wrote a book several decades ago on the experiences of folks living with chronic illnesses, such as arthritis, diabetes, emphysema, and lupus, among others, and aptly titled it *Good Days, Bad Days*.[5] That title applies to my experience with SLL and the treatment regimen, as well as to others I've known suffering with different cancers. But it holds only to a certain extent, as I have found that the good to bad gradient is more granular, with frequent fluctuation from moment to moment throughout the day, often without any clear sense of what triggered the switch. That unpredictability alone pretty much ensures that the animating condition—cancer—remains ever present in the mind. And that was pretty much assured when what limited vision that remained in my left eye would totally vanish within two weeks.

I woke up on the Tuesday after Labor Day in quite a bit of pain, and I was totally blind: no peripheral vision, no discernible light penetration, no vague object or form penetration. I sat up on the side of the bed and said—actually yelled—to Roberta, "I can't see a fucking thing out of my left eye! I'm totally blind in that eye!" Total blindness, according to the American Foundation for the Blind, is defined as "the complete lack of light perception and form perception," neither of which my left eye was able to do.[6] I felt a sense of panic, wondering what the hell was going on.

An early morning appointment with the ophthalmologist revealed "a lot of new bleeding," which was the source of the expanded visual obstruction. In order to stem the bleeding, he injected the eye once again and this time recommended that my oncologist and cardiologist consider suspending the trial medications and blood thinner so as to increase my platelet count. An exam two weeks later indicated that the bleeding had abated, so the medication suspension may have been helpful in that regard, but other than that it was not clear how much difference the suspension made. My left eye was still totally blind and becoming increasingly painful due to blood clots and mounting pressure within the eye, which registered close to 60 mm, well above the average intraocular pressure of 15, at a late afternoon mid-September appointment.

The pain continued to escalate. At times I felt like my eye was going to burst, triggering intermittent nausea and vomiting, as well as mounting exhaustion. A regimen of pain medicines (hydrocodone, morphine pills, and Tylenol), along with different types of prescribed eye drops helped to control the pain but never eliminated it. Additionally, the morphine came with its own annoying side effects, such as increasing difficulty sleeping and constipation. And none of these treatments or medications restored my vision; my left eye was still totally blind.

Given the accelerated pressure, severe pain, and the threat to the integrity of my eyeball, I was scheduled for emergency surgery that evening.

CHAPTER 9

A Blinded Eye: A Medical Anomaly?

While sitting in the hospital waiting room awaiting the assemblage of the surgical team, my ophthalmologist, who was the lead surgeon, came out to check on my condition. For some reason, the Annie Sullivan/Helen Keller story had come to mind, and I said to him, "I hope you're a miracle worker." I'm not sure what I was thinking. I had no expectation the surgery would restore my vision; that was unlikely given that the bleeding and accelerated pressure had probably irreparably damaged my retina and optic nerve. So I guess what I had in mind was that the surgery would mitigate the pain by extracting blood clots while simultaneously making sure the eyeball didn't collapse.

The surgery and general anesthesia went well. The retinal surgeon removed the recent blood clots that had formed in the vitreous in front of the retina and inserted a bubble behind the retina to try to push down the pooled clots to increase the prospect of their being absorbed into the body. I was released, and Roberta and I returned home around eleven o'clock that night. I had to sleep with my upper body and head completely upright, which I did undisturbed and comfortably for the first time in several weeks, due no doubt in part to the residue of the anesthetic I was given the previous night. But mostly, I could rest because the pain had receded to a level 1 or 2 from what had been closer to a 7+ on the 10-point subjective pain scale. And my impacted eyeball was still in place. Did these desired outcomes make the surgeon a miracle worker? I have no idea, but I was thankful for the surgical intervention, my blind eye notwithstanding. The sharp attenuation of pain and the recaptured ability to sleep without grimacing clearly elicited welcome feelings of relief.

Throughout the ongoing ordeal with the loss of vision in my left eye, the question of its causation became a gnawing one. As previously noted, the two control group drugs—ibrutinib and obinutuzumab—coupled with the blood thinner, had driven down my platelet count, thus increasing in a cascading fashion the probability of abnormal bleeding somewhere. But were they the primary cause of the eventual blindness? And why the left eye rather than the right eye or some other corporal location, like the brain? This was a gnawing curiosity, especially after I learned that a medical acquaintance had died from a brain bleed while in a trial for another variant of non-Hodgkin lymphoma.

It's not easy to answer such questions of causation. Clearly one condition for establishing a causal relationship is determining the temporal order of the variables in question. Another condition is detecting a statistical correlation between those variables. Both of these conditions appear to have been readily operative in assessing the relationship between the clinical trial and the medical issues designated as its iatrogenic side effects. Not only did the onset of the clinical trial precede the occurrence of the side effects I experienced—the tumor lysis, low platelet count, various skin issues, atrial fibrillation, and blindness in the left eye—but the statistical incidence of these and other side effects as the result of the trial drugs had already been established, with most being occasional or rare rather than common occurrences. But even if the clinical trial drugs (particularly ibrutinib and obinutuzumab) were the primary precipitants of these side effects, that didn't rule out other possible contributing factors.

In looking back at the devolving vision loss, for example, there were other complicating factors as well as the trial medications. One was the week and a half between when I first requested an appointment and when I first saw an ophthalmologist, and another two weeks after that before my initial appointment with the retinal specialist. This extended time not only delayed whatever treatment I would get, but likely reduced the chance that the treatment intervention would make any difference. Another factor was I didn't rush to the eye institute as soon as I noticed the vision impairment. I'd had some experience with eye troubles in the past; in 2004 I had two retinal detachments in my left eye. But this new impairment didn't present like those detachments, so I wasn't as insistent as I might have been about getting an immediate appointment. And neither my ophthalmologists nor my oncologist seemed alarmed at the time. The initial examining ophthalmologists indicated that the retinal bleed "might resolve itself like a bad bruise." Several weeks later in a Zoom meeting with my oncologist, I mentioned the retinal bleeding impairing the vision in my left eye. She said she had quite a bit of firsthand experience with that since it occurred among some of her leukemia patients because of their low platelet counts. "Retinal hemorrhages often resolve themselves," she added, "much like bruises do." For all of these intersecting considerations, I was probably not as alarmed as perhaps I should have been.

Further complicating my thinking were my repeated medical appointments, seemingly averaging two per week over the past year. I was tired of one medical appointment after another to see my various physicians or to get another test, most often another blood test to assess various kidney-functioning markers and my low platelet count.

One additional factor might have contributed to the bleeding. For more than a year, I had been doing fifty push-ups almost daily, not only to maintain a certain level of muscular fitness in my chest and shoulders but also to demonstrate psychologically that I wasn't about to succumb to cancer and COVID. It was another way of telling myself, "I will not let my illness(es) define me." I continued to resist making it the cloak I wore. However, when I informed a close friend who is a cardiologist, as well as my own cardiologist, about the push-ups, they concurred that I should suspend them for the time being because they can intensify intraocular pressure, increasing the prospect of bleeding. Thus, the push-ups may have been a contributing factor as well. So responsibility for the blindness in my left eye might be apportioned across a number of factors and actors, including myself.

However, my ophthalmologist and oncologist suggested otherwise. In an appointment with the ophthalmologist several weeks following the surgery while discussing my loss of vision, he stated, "I've had a few other patients lose their vision, but I've never had a case like yours. It is a medical anomaly." My oncologist also disabused me of the notion that I bore some blame for the vision loss when we met several months later to discuss the outcome of the completed clinical trial. In response to my self-incriminatory comment that the impairment might not have been so severe if I had acted more quickly, she said in no uncertain terms: "You had nothing to do with it! It was due to the effects of the trial drugs. There was nothing you could have done."

Not only were her comments reassuring, but they also reminded me that a month and a half prior to when I first noticed the visual decline, I had seen my glaucoma specialist at the eye clinic for a checkup of my vision and eye pressure, including an exam of my optic nerves and a vision field test. The various assessments indicated that all was in relatively good age-related order with my eyes, with no warnings about any forthcoming problems. So I left the clinic that day in better spirits then I had at the completion of other recent medical appointments, which accented one thing or another, like my low platelet count, ongoing skin issues, and the trial pharmacological-triggered arrhythmia.

That appointment, coupled with the self-blame assuaging comments of my physicians, would seem to exempt me from responsibility for my blind left eye. But there was still that gnawing question of whether my vision might have been salvaged if I had done something else. But I eventually came to realize that there is little point to chewing on such questions, since doing so does nothing to remedy what has transpired. What seemed clear, however, is that the inception of the clinical trial was the cascading event that triggered the sequential iatrogenic side effects, including the new blindness in my left eye.

This fifth and most traumatizing iatrogenic trial side effect also led to a loss of depth perception. Optimal depth perception, which entails seeing things in three dimensions, including size and distance, is contingent on binocular vision. Thus, having only one fully functioning eye—monocular vision—impaired me in other ways. My balance was now less than optimal, requiring me to be more guarded about turning quickly and risk falling.[1] I also found it helpful to hold on to a rail when ascending or descending stairs in case I misread the steps, something I hadn't needed to do previously. I even had to be more cautious when I walked, keeping my focus on the ground between five to ten yards ahead because I would feel slightly dizzy if I looked around at the scenery. One of my ophthalmologists emphasized something even more important. "You need to protect your good eye," he said. "Be on guard for low-hanging tree limbs and other hazards when outside and walking."

With the anomic ambiguity that persisted throughout the clinical trial, my bout with COVID, and especially now with the blinded left eye and the compromised depth perception, I was confronted with the stark realization that my AFib and particularly the vision loss were not passing aggravations. They were now permanent treatment side effects that were part of my being for the rest of my life.

The lives of those experiencing challenging illnesses, including my own, are infused with loss. As Michael Stein writes in his chapter on loss in *The Lonely Patient*, "The losses brought on by illness are endless."[2] Among the losses he chronicles include changes in physical appearance, as with disfiguring surgeries or accidents, and physical functioning, as with the loss of continence and balance. It was one thing to have to deal with them physically—like remembering to grab the railing when walking downstairs or up because of limited depth perception—but it was another matter to deal with them psychologically. Just as I had fluctuating thoughts and feelings regarding the dual cancers, trial, and COVID, I had vacillating feelings about these enduring side effects. How much say should I grant them in my daily life? How much weight should they carry? Should I allow them to intrude on my daily routines, altering how I proceeded in comparison to the past?

In my case, my appearance hadn't changed other than the mentioned weight loss, and I had little visible disfigurement unless one took a close look at my eyes. I was born with sky-blue eyes, but the color of the blind left eyeball changed over time, initially black and then becoming cloudy gray. Although I didn't think much about the change in coloration, it certainly could be construed as a loss, especially since the deep, sky-blue color of my eyes was a kind of identity marker, often eliciting complimentary comments from my grandmother and several aunts when I was younger and later from my two spouses. Some folks may have noticed the difference, but they hardly ever mentioned it. However, one day when I was out walking with one of my grandsons at a Los Angeles Rams preseason practice, I mentioned that I have a difficult time detecting people approaching on my left side. He stopped, turned around, took a focused look, and said, "I see now, the blind eyeball is black." He had made the connection between my eye's appearance and my blindness.

And another time, while ordering in a restaurant, the server said, "You have two different colored eyes. That's neat! I've never seen that before."

The oddity of the comment notwithstanding, I chuckled and said, "Yeah, but I wasn't born that way; it was because of treatment for an illness."

Occasionally, though, as I pursued my daily activities, someone might ask about my eye and vision loss, or my extended absence, that would prompt me to provide an elaborated response. For instance, late one morning as I walked into the pool locker room after a lap swim, another regular swimmer asked how I was doing, and commented, "I haven't seen you for a while." I replied that I couldn't swim for several weeks due to surgery on my blind left eye, which opened the door for him to ask further questions and for a more thorough response. But once I explained what happened and why, I emphasized that it was good to be back in the pool again, highlighting my swimmer identity rather than accenting the cancer and treatment side effects.

Even so, I increasingly found myself more reliant on Roberta for some activities, especially when accessing and driving the many overlapping freeways snaking through the LA metropolitan area. The role change, with Roberta in the driver's seat and me riding shotgun, not only eased my anxiety but also made Roberta more comfortable. Thus, when we decided to drive to northern California in October 2023—about a year after I lost vision in my left eye—to visit a granddaughter in college, Roberta took the driver's seat. During the eight-hour road trip north on Interstate 5, I suggested to Roberta, who had been driving for five hours straight, that she pull over and let me drive a bit to give her a break and maybe grab a quick nap. Anyone who has driven north of LA on Interstate 5 to or past the San Francisco and Sacramento exits knows that it is filled with semitrucks trailing, almost bumper to bumper, or passing one another. This proved particularly challenging for me as I took over the wheel. Being blind in the left eye meant that I had to turn my head a little more than 90 degrees to the left to see my options when pulling into the passing lane. This meant I had to momentarily take my good eye off the vehicle in front of me, thus increasing the odds of rear-ending it if it suddenly slowed or stopped, especially so with my impaired depth-perception. This was somewhat of tense and stressful experience for me, as well for Roberta, who never did close her eyes to catch a wink. She unsurprisingly suggested, after about thirty minutes, that I pull over so she could resume driving. I didn't resist or argue; in fact, I was quite happy to reclaim the passenger seat.

As I negotiated this new way of being, what I came to realize is that I harbored a good deal of unease about using the illness identity card and the extent to which doing so would accent its importance vis-à-vis other personal identities. This identity confusion was underscored each time I attended the monthly virtual CLL support group meetings. The meetings were helpfully informative in learning about CLL and the journeys of fellow travelers. But listening to their experiences for two hours made me feel as though the CLL/SLL identity card was being stamped and certified, thereby highlighting its salience.

Maybe the ongoing anomic ambiguity and associated identity confusion I experienced were due in no small part to my resistance to accepting all that I had been dealing with and my fear of what might wait for me down the road. At its core, I came to realize, was my resistance to letting everything I was going through impose an unwanted identity upon me. I never talked to a therapist throughout the journey, but if I had I would conjecture that she would have said something about denial and resistance.

I'd continue navigating these shifting feelings and my precarious sense of identity as my time in the clinical trial came to a close.

CHAPTER 10

The Clinical Trial Ends

I was much relieved when I finally made it to the last day in the clinical trial in mid-October 2022. It culminated fifteen months of the trial itself and the daily regimen of two sets of different targeted therapy pills, one of which had been miraculous in terms of its reduction in the size of the impacted lymph nodes while simultaneously brutal in terms of its cascading iatrogenic side effects.

Such feelings of relief—whether in response to the nonoccurrence of a worrisome diagnosis or procedure, or to the cessation of pain, a treatment regimen, or a troubling illness—surfaced at various junctures during my illness odyssey, providing two important psychological functions. For me and others on similar paths, they reduced the anxiety that comes from the uncertainties of illness, particularly of the more vexing and shape-shifting kind such as cancer; and they paved the way for dealing with the next challenge by reminding travelers along this road that relief, in some form or another, may be a forthcoming and assuredly soothing companion.

The day was a busy one, as I was scheduled for blood work and three contrast-based CT scans for the neck, chest, and abdomen, followed by an appointment with the oncology nurse practitioner for a palpation lymph node exam and an excision of bone marrow from my left hip. As we drove to the medical center, I felt a sense of anticipatory relief but guarded about allowing myself to experience full-blown relief given the various exams that awaited me.

The NP's palpation revealed nothing enlarged or suspicious, which the initial reads of the chest scan confirmed. The blood draw results were also good, revealing no concerning markers. All that remained was the bone marrow tap, which would be the most trying exam of the day.

As the nurses prepped me for the bone marrow tap—considered the gold standard exam for assessing whether there is any residual cancer in the marrow—the clinical trial coordinator and NP ran into the private room where I sat, excitedly reporting that the chest scan did, in fact, look normal, with no oversized lymph nodes. Obviously, this was great news, but these initial results were not definitive. For that, we would have to await the lab results of the bone marrow excision, which would be several weeks away.

In prep for the tap, the attending nurse specialist injected me with a dose of morphine and anesthetized my hip with several shots of lido-caine to mute the otherwise likely prospect of severe pain. Knowing that didn't seem to make much difference in my anticipation of what might be forthcoming, however. I lay on my stomach on the exam table, and the nurse pressed her weight heavily on the syringe to make sure that the excision needle penetrated my hip bone and accessed the marrow. As she asked ongoing questions of "How are you doing?" and "Are you feeling any pain?" I had this dreadful feeling that teeth-clenching pain would manifest itself any second. Although I mainly felt the weight of the nurse pushing on the syringe rather than bone penetration, the palpable sense of anticipatory pain prompted me to clench the bed rails beneath the mattress. Beads of sweat dripped down my forehead as she retracted the excision needle and announced that the tap was near completion. As I continued to lie there while the nurse bandaged the targeted area, I was reminded how the anticipation of pain can be nearly as excruciating as its actual occurrence, something that I knew intellectually but not so much experientially until this occasion. In any case, as I got up, I felt relief in two senses: that the excision ordeal was over, and that the pain was more anticipatory than actual.

During the excision procedure, Roberta sat in the room observing, but not with comfort. She saw what I could not, such as the circumference and length of the excision needle—similar to the size of a pencil. But when the attending nurse pressed with her body weight on the handle of the excision needle syringe, Roberta sensed my anticipatory distress, which contributed to her own discomfort. That Roberta couldn't reach out and hold a hand or swab my forehead, that she couldn't do anything but grit her teeth like I did, exacerbated her empathetic torment. Such is the way with loving, care-giving partners, isn't it? Your pain is theirs, and vice versa.

So, at times like this, the quality of the relief I experienced, for example, was not only a function of that which triggered it, whether cancellation or completion of an unwelcome procedure or the receipt of good news. It was also augmented by the fact that it was shared. In every instance, I didn't experience my relief alone; a core of significant others felt it too. We didn't just share these occasions of relief; we also shared uncertainty, corresponding anxieties, and even pain.

Even with Roberta at my side, and the relief of reaching the end of the clinical trial, anger would bubble to the surface much like a percolating volcano. And when the feeling of anger did surface, it wasn't of the highly combustible kind, but it still felt quite gripping and consuming. It sometimes emerged at unexpected or inconvenient times, such as during the period when I awaited the results of the bone marrow tap.

In the morning in late October 2022, a week after the final day of the trial and about a month after my emergency eye surgery, Roberta and I went for a three-mile walk. I felt a simmering anger for most of the walk, which escalated toward the end. I wanted to be alone and went off in a different direction from Roberta and our dog. I wasn't angry at anyone in particular. Rather, it was just a feeling of being mad without a specific target. I was especially irritated about my eye, feeling anxious about the impending report on the bone marrow biopsy, and fuming about an upcoming series of exams and discussions regarding my AFib.

I suppose I felt a bit sorry for myself as well. Not only was I totally blind in one eye, but I had this ongoing sensation that a part of me was missing. The eye was still intact, even though the color of the eyeball had changed, but most annoying was the absence of any hint of vision or penetrating light. It felt a bit like I had lost a sidekick who had been riding shotgun on a lifelong road trip and I was now trying to come to grips with the realization that the reliant sidekick was no longer there. No longer could I ask my sidekick if his eye registered what I thought I was seeing. Is that really a big rig barreling over the hill on the horizon, or is it an illusion? Am I seeing what I think I'm seeing? Or even more alarming, am I not seeing what I should be seeing?

This latter concern was accented during my walk. As I often do, I was walking on the side of the asphalt street rather than on the concrete sidewalk because asphalt is a bit softer and easier on your body than concrete. Rather than looking around, I steadied my focus about fifteen feet ahead on the ground or street, which my ophthalmologist recommended, and which also stabilized my balance. But as I looked ahead ten feet or so as I approached a parked landscaping truck with tools extending over the rear tailgate, I initially failed to see a long pole sticking out at head level well beyond the other tools and came within inches of jamming my forehead into it. This close encounter, due to my impaired depth perception, was not only alarming but also made me mad—mad about the near accident, mad about the blind eye and compromised depth perception, and mad about how once routinized aspects of life had now changed. It also reminded me that I must be ever vigilant with no sidekick to give me another read on what I was seeing or not.

This growing realization, coupled with the angst about the clinical trial results and the upcoming cardiological exams and consultation, seemed more than sufficient to account for the anger. When I returned home, I apologized to Roberta for going off on my own, noting that I just felt angry about all of "this shit." She said she understood fully, as she always seemed to do. "You've been dealing with a lot," she added, "and still are." What she didn't add though, is that she had been dealing with it all as well, which added another source of angst for me as well as her.

Intermittent anger continued to percolate and seep into my daily life, but it was noncombustible, maybe because it was highly predictable. It was triggered, almost always, by problems generated by the blind left eye and my lack of trustworthy depth perception in the course of performing routinized daily activities. For example, I could be chopping or dicing vegetables for a salad, all of which I couldn't see clearly, and realize that I needed a set of glasses but couldn't find the right one. What was once a routine, almost habituated task was now challenging. Sometimes, when walking from one room to another, I would turn the corner too quickly, not seeing the wall on the left, and bump and bruise my left shoulder or scrape my forearm against the corner. The bump and scrape made me mad, but far more aggravating was the realization that I had to navigate my way around my own house with caution. Such moments predictably sparked a flash of anger, but never of the raging kind. Maybe a few slapdash curses, but I never slammed any doors, punched a wall, or threw anything within reach. I did come to realize, though, that these ongoing but sporadic flares of restrained anger were, for the time being, a frustrating accompaniment of the blind left eye.

It prompted me to wonder if the anger I felt was related to grieving the total loss of vision in my left eye. In 1969, Elisabeth Kübler-Ross's seminal book *On Death and Dying* introduced the five stages of grief to the popular discourse, with the five stages being denial, anger, bargaining, depression, and acceptance.[1] I can't say that her five-stage thesis resonated fully with me when dealing with the loss of my late wife, Judy. I experienced denial for only a couple of months, and anger periodically, but never bargaining or debilitating depression. I eventually came to acceptance, but not in the sense of feeling that the loss was okay but in the sense that I could move on and even come to hold another woman's hand and fall in love again. So, I now found myself wondering if I was experiencing similar feelings regarding my newfound blind eye. I had read about the grief often associated with the loss of a limb and its similarity to the grief caused by the death of a loved one.[2] And I knew experientially from my late wife's two mastectomies that she not only experienced a sense of loss, but that the double-edged loss also had a profound effect on her body image. Not so surprising, I guess, that I would be grieving my vision and my ability to perform tasks that I once took for granted without interruption, accident, and perhaps injury.

Another significant loss that permeated my experience but is likely to be glossed over in most discussions of illness-related losses is the loss of time. Several widely repeated quotes, attributed to the likes of Benjamin Franklin and Winston Churchill, refer to time as an invaluable resource that can't be retrieved or hoarded. One thing that is certain about serious, prolonged illnesses and injuries is that they consume, indeed devour, time. Time in emergency rooms, time in the hospital, time in infusion labs, time getting blood drawn, time getting scans or MRIs, time in pharmacies picking up drug prescriptions, time in one physician's office after another, time in the car driving to and from these various appointments, and time recuperating or shielding oneself at home, often in isolation due to some contagious ailment like COVID or vulnerability to it.

These weeks, months, and years eaten up by serious illness and accidents and their treatment regimens adds to a huge loss of time that I could have been spent in more fulfilling ways, like spending more fun time with my wife, children, grandchildren, and other relatives and friends, particularly on meaningful occasions. During the few times I was hospitalized and while I was saddled with COVID for forty-five days, I often found myself slipping into reveries about what I would be doing with that time if I weren't so confined. Much of what I imagined, such as special occasions like holidays and birthdays, I did experience again because of their recurrence, but the times I missed could never be retrieved beyond my imagination because they had been lost with the passage of time consumed by illness and the various treatment regimens.

Yet, since Roberta was always with me throughout all of the seemingly endless medical appointments, we probably spent more time together with the same focus of attention than at any point in our relationship. In this regard, we didn't lose time, we simply consumed time together differently. Moreover, we rarely thought of these medically nested times together as squandered. Rather, we found that these times enriched the depth and durability of our commitment to each other. This is not to say that we didn't sometimes lament the lost time and opportunities to pursue more pleasurable activities together. On our way home from one appointment after another, we would sometimes imagine what we might be doing if it weren't for the trial-based requisite appointments. Maybe we'd be strolling through art galleries or museums in Paris or Amsterdam, or getting lost in a unique bookstore in London, or driving along California's Pacific Coast Highway and pulling over for an afternoon hike. Whatever we imagined, though, we imagined it together. We thus came to understand these time-consuming medical appointments as congealing into a unique kind of bonding experience rather than as an unforgiving time sink.

Now, twenty days after the final day of the clinical trial, fifteen and a half months since the clinical trial began, and five years and one month since my initial diagnosis of lymphoma, Roberta and I anxiously awaited the appointment with my oncologist. Today we would learn the definitive results of the battery of three CT scans and the bone marrow biopsy, and assess the outcome of the trial.

On the way to the appointment, Roberta and I commented that we both felt a bit of trepidation. We knew from prior scans and hands-on examinations for oversized lymph nodes that the most severely impacted nodes in the abdomen and pelvic area had declined in size significantly, but we didn't know whether some of the nodes still harbored cancerous cells. Moreover, we had yet to hear anything about the bone marrow probe. Besides, we had become almost accustomed to receiving bad news considering the iatrogenic side effects of the clinical trial medications, especially with my heart and left eye. Additionally, we remembered the psychologically tormented wait to see my oncology urologist back in October 2017 for the lab results of the surgically excised lymph node (and the bladder tumor excised two weeks earlier) to determine what kind of lymphoma I might have. I had also been on this posttreatment journey with Judy many times before, driving her to her oncologist and radiologists to assess the results of her latest chemo-infusion and radiation treatment. Given these past postexam assessments with Judy, it is hardly surprising that I recalled those experiences, which amplified my already heightened anxiety.

So it was with this shared anxiety that Roberta and I sat in an exam office awaiting the oncologist's knock on the exam room door. After an initial exchange of pleasantries, and her review of my overall medical situation, she said, thinking we had already learned of the results of the bone marrow puncture, "You must be happy with the lab results." We indicated that we hadn't seen or heard the actual results. "Well," she said with surprise and exuberance, "there is *no* cancer in the bone marrow." She also noted that the lab tests looked for residual cancer in ten thousand cells and found "not a trace." She added, "If the lymphoma were to come back, it would be many years."

We were not expecting the worst, as noted earlier, but this was the best news possible. Complete remission, with a favorable prognosis going forward! We were elated, almost to the point of being overwhelmed. In fact, I was so relieved and excited that I asked the oncologist if we could fist-bump, which we did with big smiles.

Roberta and I walked out of the exam room to the check-out desk to make a follow-up appointment in three months, and I told the oncologist, "I suspect that good reports like I just received must make you and the oncology team almost as happy as the recipient client."

"Absolutely," she said. "It makes our day too."

As Roberta and I returned to the parking structure, tears began streaming down my face. They were the good kind of tears—tears of joy, which had been too few over the past five years. Clearly, it was an occasion of ecstatic relief for both Roberta and me.

CHAPTER 11

Remission and Cancer Consciousness

One rule of cancer that I've learned is that it is like a fixated interrogator:
It does not allow you to change subjects—when you think you can.

—SIDDHARTHA MUKHERJEE[1]

Hearing you've attained complete remission is great news, but it doesn't mean you're cured. As noted earlier, it means that there is no detectable evidence of what is called minimal or measurable residual disease (MRD). You feel relieved, to be sure, but not without concern since you're back in a state of active observation, sometimes depressingly called "watch and wait" or "watch and worry." The cancer is still likely to be embedded in your consciousness because of its unpredictability and the variable likelihood of its recurrence depending on such contingencies as the type and stage of the cancer, the patient's overall health condition, the treatment options and their tolerability, and the existence of treatment-induced side effects that themselves require a new regimen of observation and treatment. Accordingly, concern, indeed fear, about recurrence seldom fades completely for those in remission. The odyssey continues without a determinate ending in sight.

Particularly troubling for me was when I was reminded, during a CLL support group discussion, that you fall back into the "watch and wait" status when in remission. This I knew, as I suspect most cancer patients do. But highlighting it reminded me that I would likely be carrying this identity card for the rest of my life, with the very real prospect of it being activated in the event of relapse and pressed into a position of identity prominence. The phrase "watch and wait" thus struck me as a psychologically troubling way to frame one's postremission status. It was like saying, metaphorically, that you have won a major battle, but the war continues, and it is therefore likely that you will have other battles to wage down the road; so, stay alert. No doubt I hoped that remission meant I was just passing through this landscape of illness, but support group meetings, however well intended, and the capricious character of cancer conspired to suggest otherwise.

Thus, there are too many factors at play to presume that cancer's remission, even if long term, will relax its hold on consciousness. The fear of its relapse may recede into the closets of the backstage of consciousness, but any number of provocations can readily amplify and recall it: a nagging sore, a set of monitoring exams and the wait for their results, a physician's call, and the "how are you doing" questions by significant others and acquaintances who have learned of your odyssey. For example, Judy was in long-term remission for fifteen years, but not without the concern of recurrence. Every mammogram, blood test, or scan generated renewed anxiety that manifested itself in a worried face and a kind of restlessness until the good news results muted the unease and pushed the concern about recurrence into the backwater of consciousness until the next round of tests. And this anxious waiting for good news results not only manifested itself in my late wife but also among our three children, who almost always noticed their mother's anxiety and mine, thus illustrating the social and psychological metastatic character of cancer. That's one of the gnawing things about cancer. Although it is concentrated physically within the patient, it typically radiates psychologically throughout the patient's immediate network, thus embedding itself in the consciousness of the patient's significant others.

And this is often the case even after the patient has expired due to the fear of susceptibility because of the possible heritability of cancerous genetic mutations. Such fear was accented in our adult daughters, who worried about inheriting the lineage of breast cancer on their mother's side, which not only afflicted Judy but also her sister and her mother. A comprehensive BRCA genetic test, which assesses vulnerability to breast cancer, found no deleterious mutation in Judy's BRCA1 or BRCA2 genes, thereby diluting the prospect of its heritability. But their mother's dual experiences, along with those of their aunt, grandmother, and great-grandmother, were sufficiently worrisome to prompt our daughters to join a university hospital breast cancer clinic for ongoing monitoring as well as push one of them to have a preventive bilateral mastectomy. Clearly the fear of cancer was in the front stage of their consciousness. Such is the nature of the psychological metastasis of cancer.

One morning a few days after my oncologist informed Roberta and me that I was now in remission, Roberta and I were walking and I said something that prompted her to say, "You can't play the cancer card anymore." She was joking, of course, especially since she had been far more likely than me to inform others of my condition. In any case, her joking reference to the "cancer card" triggered thoughts about the so-called "sick role" and my psychological and functional adjustment now that I was in remission and that role was no longer applicable.

The "sick role," as a medical sociologist like Roberta would know well, denotes the reduced everyday responsibilities of those medically designated as ill.[2] As with all social roles, like that of physician or nurse, there are culturally normative rights and obligations associated with it. Thus, those encumbered by a medically legitimated illness have the right to be excused from their usual social duties and obligations, to receive care and deference from others that corresponds to the character of illness they suffer, and to be free of blame for their illness. The flip side of those role-based rights is the obligation to facilitate recovery by pursuing the culturally recommended standard-of-care practices and treatments. We have all been the beneficiaries of these rights many times over, as when we have been excused from school or work because of a cold, the flu, COVID, or some noncommunicable illness like cancer. It was such exemptions that Roberta had in mind when she said I couldn't play the "cancer card" anymore, given the recent report that my SLL variant of lymphoma was in remission.

For the person in remission, as well, the relationship between one's physical condition and thoughts and feelings about relapse are often uncertain and untidy, thus making remission a tricky medical designation and pretty much assuring that cancer is lingering in one's consciousness. So yes, the remission verdict may take the cancer card out of play as a normatively acceptable justification for exemption from certain social responsibilities, but not out of consciousness. The cancer may wane and even disappear, but consciousness of it not so likely, even if my dreams of losing my internal compass—and losing Judy and Roberta—abated after the clinical trial ended.

Additionally, even if one's treatment regimen drives one's cancer into remission, the existence of unresolved iatrogenic side effects may well keep the sick role in play in different ways. For me, the AFib and vision loss in my left eye are not only troublesome in their own right but are also permanent and ever-present embodied reminders of the cancer treatment regimen that triggered their occurrence. This is particularly the case with the vision loss and compromised depth perception and how it has altered and complicated the doing of various daily activities I previously took for granted.

One of these activities, reading, was impacted, in part because one eye was doing the work that the two formerly functional eyes had done separately or together. What's more, I now had four sets of glasses to juggle: one for close-up, as when reading printed material; another for intermediate distance, as when looking at the computer screen; a third for distance, as when driving or seeing more sharply what is on the television screen; and another for being outdoors in the bright sun. I now found that prolonged reading, especially without focused light, was more trying, and that switching glasses when looking back and forth between the computer screen and textual material on the desk was often frustrating. Both were annoying developments given that my career work, even though I had retired, largely depends on reading and writing.

Another daily activity that had been negatively impacted by the cancer and its treatment side effects was, of course, driving. One of my friends—with whom I'd been sharing my odyssey via email and telephone—commented in one email exchange that he was especially struck by my reference to the loss of my left eye as the loss of a "trusted sidekick" and how it resonated with a recent experience of his. After sharing that he recently had cataract surgery that had affected his own vision temporarily, including a frustrating reduction in his depth perception, during which he also sometimes walked into things that he simply hadn't seen, he asked, "It makes me wonder how safe you feel driving now, and how the potential loss of ability to drive impacts your sense of self." This was a poignant question since driving comfortably, without heightened awareness, now appeared to be a thing of the past.

As my friend suspected, such experiences and the decline in my confidence to drive safely in some circumstances did impact my sense of self somewhat. But it wasn't because cars or the cars I drove were ever of great personal import; for me, cars were always about going from point A to Z rather than a significant masculine signpost, as cars are for many men. Still, I sometimes found myself wondering what others might think as they saw me get into the front passenger seat with Roberta on the driver's side and with her hands on the wheel. Would they wonder if I was disabled, which I was visually? Or might they think I was an old man with my wife or even daughter driving, or perhaps I was just a lousy driver or had too much to drink? Such curiosities seemed silly in some respects, but that they did surface on occasion suggested some unease about how I might be seen by others in certain circumstances.

My friend also wondered more generally how I was affected by the potential loss of some autonomy and my feelings related to having others do things for me that I had almost always done for myself. This pointed query struck a responsive chord. The driving issue was only one case in point. Indeed, I did feel a loss of self-sufficiency and independence because of not being able to do some tasks that I had done previously without difficulty or a second thought. As a consequence, I found myself seeking out new compensatory devices and stratagems.

One such compensatory adjustment was getting a handicap parking permit. Roberta suggested that I should get one because it would make it easier for me to park, given the blind left eye and lack of depth perception made it difficult to pull into tight parking places between two cars. My ophthalmologist agreed. "Absolutely," he said. We got one, but with some reluctance on my part. I knew it could be beneficial when I was driving and needed to park, but I also saw it as a kind of symbolic crutch signifying an identity status I clearly had trouble claiming as my own.

Even when walking for exercise, I am now more conscious, more aware of what's in front of me and on the lookout for obstacles and hazards like low-hanging branches that could smash into my good eye. When hiking, I now use hiking poles to help compensate for my impaired depth-perception and thus judge whether there is more of a step up or down than I can accurately gauge. When walking in public places with Roberta, I am more conscious of bumping into other pedestrians or shoppers and thus remind her to walk on my left to lessen the odds of my banging into one or more of them passing by on that side. And if someone I am meeting or know sticks out their hand to shake or fist-bump, I now look as closely as I can to make sure that I connect with the extended hand rather than air. Even when I'm home and chopping up a mixture of vegetables for a salad, braise, or stew, I am not only much more conscious where my fingers are in relation to the chopping knife, but I often wear, at Roberta's insistence, a protective glove on my left hand to reduce the odds of slicing a finger in case the knife slips. And I no longer walk through the house unaware of the walls or right-angled counter corners because I've bumped into and scraped my arms against them too many times. In many respects I have become more familiar with aspects of everyday life that I had taken for granted and am now navigating them in ways that I hadn't thought about before. Such increased awareness and the development of compensatory adjustments are unsurprisingly common not only among more severely visually impaired individuals but among most individuals handicapped by various disabilities. Each of the associated effects of the blinded left eye were, like the eye itself, now enduring features of my life.

The functionless eye is simply there, contributing nothing to my negotiation of everyday life other than what I experience as a kind of signaling interference occasioned by very bright lights—as with the more luminous car headlights, particularly on SUVs and pickup trucks—that are penetrating enough to signal the brain that the eye is trying to see, even though it sees nothing I can discern. One of my ophthalmologists explained, "There may be one or two remaining photoreceptors on the retina that pick up some light, even though the retina is nonfunctional." Consequentially, the "out there" remains pitch black, from that eye's vantage point, except for the pin-prick specks of intruding, unsettling light that I discovered can be muffled with an eye patch. I thus keep an eye patch at the ready in my pocket to strap on whenever I sense light-inducing signaling interference, as when encountering fluctuating brightness in places such as airport corridors or my ophthalmologist's brightly lit examining room.

Besides the visual functional utility of the eye patch, it also functions something akin to an attention magnet, drawing looks and occasional comments from passers-by, acquaintances, and even sometimes intimates. "You look dashing," several acquaintances have told me. I don't recall Roberta using that phrase, but she often reminds me to put on the eye patch when going out, prompting me to ask if she thought I looked more debonair with the patch than without. "Of course not," she predictably replies, but rarely without adding that I "look good" with it on. I also discovered that the eye patch functions as a signaling device in another way, suggesting to those around me in public places to give me more clearance, a little more elbow room to pass by or through. Clearly, it seems to be a semiotic indicator of some degree of disability, function-ing something like the white cane of the thoroughly blind, although not as poignantly.

Increasing awareness of the eye patch's various interactional functions prompted concern that my use of it might become a habit. But to date I only use it when I feel the need to quiet the sensed signaling interfer-ence stimulated by intermittent, fleeting, minuscule light penetration in the otherwise functionless blinded eye. Rarely, however, does anyone ask me about why I'm wearing an eye patch because, I suspect, of the

social impropriety of asking others about their visible physical limitations or impediments. That said, it attracts passing looks of curiosity,
particularly from children. Roberta and I have overheard children on
a couple of occasions say to a parent, "Look, Mommy, a pirate," and,
"There's a cyclops."

The one memorable exception occurred in mid-March 2023, when
Roberta and I were checking in at a nearby airport for our first commercial
flight since mid-February, 2020. We hadn't scheduled any trips since then
because of the intersection of COVID, my being immunocompromised,
and the clinical trial. So we looked forward to our first trip, via air, outside
of the state in three years. But as we checked in and walked to the gate,
I felt somewhat awkward, probably because that's how I looked wearing
an eye patch and, because I had recently pulled a muscle in my left thigh,
limping with the help of a cane. It was notable how other travelers moved
aside and gave us wide passage as we wound our way through the airport.
Was it the eye patch? The cane? Or a combination of the two markers
of some degree of disability? Given that travelers nodded respectfully as
I passed, I surmised that perhaps they thought I was a veteran. And sure
enough, while standing at the gate awaiting the call to board, a fellow
traveler asked me if I was, in fact, a veteran. "Yes," I responded, and
thinking that he probably thought the two impairments were the result
of my service, I added, "Neither the impaired eye nor the limp is due to
my time in the military." We talked a bit more, during which I noted,
"The limp was due to a muscle pull and the impaired eye to a treatment
side effect for a medical condition." He said he was sorry about the side
effect but added, "You look like you are adjusting well." About then, the
call to board was made, and the stranger parted, saying, "Good luck and
thank you for your service."

Did these various losses, from the physical visual ones to those impact-
ing aspects of my everyday functioning, affect my sense of autonomy and

self-concept, as my friend asked in one of our several exchanges? Given the significant adjustments I've had to make, the differences in how people sometimes perceive me, and my increased dependence on Roberta for a number of things and on other adaptive stratagems, it would seem clear that my senses of autonomy and self-concept have been affected, but only to a degree. It is not that my core conception of self has changed. I still see myself as a broadly compassionate, intelligent person, but I also see myself as more vulnerable and dependent, less self-sufficient, in some ways for some things, than before the odyssey began. So the changing aspects of the "doing" of my everyday life, including my compensatory adjustments, serve as ongoing reminders of the odyssey, functioning to embed cancer and the trial effects in my consciousness, albeit sometimes backstage and other times front stage.

But I wouldn't have navigated these changes and associated frustrations as I have without a strong network of social support.

CHAPTER 12

The Indispensability of Social Support

Of the many lessons I have learned or been reminded of in this illness odyssey, none has been more poignantly accented than the importance of social support. Broadly considered, social support encompasses the provision of emotional, informational, and tangible or instrumental assistance, along with positive appraisals, to those in need. And it is generally understood as an important facilitator of positive physical and mental health. This is not only one of the most persistent findings within the sociological study of health and medicine,[1] but it's also understood experientially by most folks dealing with serious medical issues, whether of their own or of loved ones.

Supportive social relationships are most often associated with "significant others," typically understood as close family and friends. But my experience—based not only on my journey into the landscape of illness but also on the journeys of late family members—identifies a broader base of social support. It includes those we count as our core significant others, of course, but it also recognizes a set of relational connections or allies that extend outward, much like the layers of an onion. They include what I call anchored social relationships and their fleeting cousins, anchored professionals, and spiritual/religious allies. Together with significant others, they comprise a web of intersecting modalities of support.

Foremost among my significant others was my wife, Roberta, who was with me and by my side throughout my intersecting ordeal with cancer, COVID, and the clinical trial and its iatrogenic side effects. She not only accompanied me for every appointment and procedure, devised a daily check-off system for monitoring my daily intake of fourteen pills, and reactivated her RN training and experience whenever needed, but also her expression of concern and relief paralleled mine throughout the odyssey, strengthening my spirit and resolve. Her multifaceted support also included driving me to my seemingly endless appointments and tests, sitting in for each appointment, asking questions and taking notes, and allocating whatever time these and other mentioned supportive activities devoured. This shared relief, anxiety, and pain weren't all that characterized the depth of her support; so did her accommodating willingness to be pulled into the time sink that the treatment and negotiation of my cancer and clinical trial mandated.

Sometimes, Roberta's unwavering support triggered flashbacks to Judy's final bedridden months and the around-the-clock attentive care the children and I provided. I was available for the better part of each day, except for the few times a week I would rush to the university to teach a class. On one of those occasions, a colleague asked, "Why don't you hire someone to take care of her? It would make it easier for you."

I replied, "Why would I do that when I am fully capable of taking care of her with my own two hands? Besides, she's been my wife for thirty-seven years, and I can provide her with the loving care that no hired caregiver can." Of course, professional, paid, nonfamily caregivers, whether in one's home or a nursing facility, can provide a number of forms of support, but they're rarely equipped to offer the range and depth of emotional support that loving significant others can provide. In addition, hired caregivers don't provide instrumental, financial assistance, which family members and friends can and may do. This is not to depreciate the value and expanding need of professional caregiving in an aging country. Rather, it is to accent the breadth and depth of caregiving provided by able, loving significant others. It is that kind of caregiving that Roberta provided.

Roberta even functioned as an information hub for my three adult children and four siblings, a handful of close friends, and strands of social relational connections beyond my core of significant others. My children lived relatively close, only thirty to sixty minutes away depending on traffic, but because of their work and school schedules, we only saw the three of them, their partners, and our grandchildren once or twice a month, except during my forty-five-day affliction with COVID. In between visits, after each physician appointment or procedure, Roberta would text my children with a summary of what transpired, the results, if any, and how I was doing. The kids would typically respond, depending on the temper of the text, with a complementary emoji and a couple of encouraging words, often followed later in the day with a telephone call. They wanted more prognostic detail of the favorable kind than the texts usually provided, but they generally responded to whatever they heard by putting a positive spin on it, saying, "You're doing great, Dad" or, "It's not as bad as it could be" or by normalizing a symptomatic complaint like tiredness and fatigue with, "I've been experiencing that too." They were sometimes right, but it was my sense that their supportive comments frequently represented an attempt to reassure themselves that their dad was going to be just fine. After all, they had already lost their mother almost two decades ago. But it is my guess that this is how kids typically respond when confronted with a parent's illness. They understandably want reassurance that things are going to be okay, so they are inclined to focus on and accent the good news results and reports. At least that was my experience.

My four siblings, three in Ohio and one in Massachusetts, also appreciated Roberta's round-by-round updates. The likelihood of face-to-face contact with my siblings was even more limited because they all lived thousands of miles away. They regularly expressed their concerns and support via phone calls, most often from my two sisters, particularly the older one who was an RN and former hospice nurse. She also had special interest in my experience, because for more than a decade, her sister-in-law had been undergoing treatment, based on a phase 1 trial, for the same B cell cancer. Being the oldest sibling with an especially supportive disposition also cast her into the role of the family "mother hen" long before our mother died in 2013. My siblings and I all could lean on her and comfortably did so. That heightened standing in the sibling pecking order notwithstanding, I think we all felt we could lean on each other when we needed an extra boost. Given our closeness, the calls were always a source of support. And it was never so much about the particulars of what was said. It was the call itself. The contact. Simply knowing they were there and that they cared. That's what mattered. I'm not surprised that during my first night in the hospital after being diagnosed with two cancers, as I feared being on the cusp of a downward slide, that I wanted to call my four siblings first thing in the morning.

Even when my siblings and my children did visit me, they didn't need to provide other streams of support beyond their emotional support. Roberta and I weren't in need of financial, instrumental support given our PPO Medicare insurance and the clinical trial coverage of the expensive targeted therapies. I wasn't bedridden and/or physically or mentally incapacitated, so I didn't need much physical support beyond what Roberta and my medical teams provided. Nor did Roberta and I look to my children and siblings for helpful information about my variant of cancer and the clinical trial, even though they would sometimes offer such information based on the experiences of their friends' parents. Rather, we relied on the clinical trial team, available CLL and leukemia/lymphoma websites, and our own reading of medical journal articles and reputable medical websites like the Mayo Clinic's to learn as much as we could, or wanted to know, about my condition and treatment.

Clearly, the support provided by my children and siblings, and a few close friends, wasn't of the instrumental, physical, or informational variety. Instead, it was purely emotional, which is the kind of support that is most strongly associated with positive health outcomes. As emphasized in a summary essay on factors accounting for variation in health and health inequalities: "People who have intimate, confiding relationships with others, and who feel they are loved and cared for, report better health and report fewer damaging effects of stress."[2] Such was the character of the support provided from Roberta, my children, my siblings, and from a few close friends.

I had a handful of male friends—most of them colleagues from my various academic appointments over the past forty or so years—who also functioned as significant others, given that they called or texted to inquire how I was doing. I always appreciated their messages and calls, because they pulled me out of my quasi-isolated world, especially when I was burdened with COVID and the clinical trial. They provided an occasion for talking about this or that with someone other than immediate family or physicians. I generally provided an outline of what was going on with my condition and treatment, but rarely did we talk much about the details. Rather, I would try to flip the inquiry in their direction, asking how they were doing, after which our discussion would likely turn to family, work—if they were still employed—or politics and sports. This character of our conversations was probably due in part to my reluctance to focus on my cancer and treatment. I wanted to talk about something else. But I suspect it was also in keeping with the general tendency for male friendships to be based more on shared activities and interests than on disclosure of personal problems or feelings, which is more common in women's friendships. Indeed, two recent national surveys of friendship showed that women are much more likely to talk about family life, their physical well-being, and mental health than men, and share their feelings more intimately.[3] Still, I valued the supportive but less confidential conversations with my handful of male friends. However, I found that conversations with a couple of these male friends—husbands of Roberta's friends—tended to be more open to mutual disclosure and expression of feelings. This was probably due to mutual sharing between Roberta and their spouses and that we often socialized as couples; we knew more about each other both individually and as couples.

Social support also emerged for me outside the core of significant others, usually anchored in a set of recurring relationships and activities in a particular place and time. For some people, those contexts can include yoga and Pilates studios, exercise gyms, and coffee shops and bars like the Boston "Cheers" pub of television fame. A 2021 survey on the "state of American friendship" indicated that most friendships are of this sort; that is, they are situational friendships.[4] Rarely do these place-specific relationships involving a limited set of activities spill into other settings or evolve into transituational friendships.[5] They can, however, be a source of considerable social support. Two variants of such anchored social support surfaced during my experience. One was nested in what can be called anchored gatherings, the other in anchored professionals.

One such place that was a source of supportive anchored relationships for me was the nearby swimming pool where Roberta and I had been doing our morning lap swimming three days a week for the past ten years. Over time, not only was there reciprocal engagement among "the regulars"—those who usually swam in the same time frame—but some of us also came to know each other on a first-name basis and shared personal information. And this seemed particularly true of the women swimmers, including Roberta, who would share information with other regulars when they inquired about my condition based on their observations of my physical appearance (such as my protruding abdomen) and labored swimming as my cancer progressed. Roberta would tell me that so-and-so asked, "What's going on with Dave?" as they noted that my physical appearance had changed or that my swimming had "slowed" and become "choppy." Roberta would provide a thumbnail sketch of what was going on while chatting in the shallow end of the pool or changing in the women's shower room. Thereafter, as I walked from the locker room to the pool or adjusted my goggles after jumping in, one of the informed regulars would yell out to me, "Good to see you here, Dave. Keep it up." It was almost a kind of cheerleading support. Later, once my enlarged abdomen had begun to recede shortly after initiating the clinical trial and I was back in the pool, other swimmers would give me encouraging comments, like, "Your stomach has really shrunk" or "You're looking great." These comments were offered mainly from women swimmers with whom Roberta had developed a casual anchored relationship.

My connections with a few of the male regulars were of a different order. Some were more personal and detailed, due in no small part to sharing the same pre- and postswim locker room. I learned that one regular was negotiating a long battle with prostate cancer (to which he succumbed during my writing of this book), the father of a younger regular had suffered from cancer, and another fellow was born blind in one eye. Sharing and discussing our overlapping conditions generated supportive connections that manifested themselves in mutual cordiality, including inquiring about each other's well-being when our swims coincided. But our supportive camaraderie was confined to the swimming facility. Like anchored relationships in general, these did not cross over to other social spaces or places.

Sometimes, however, anchored relationships do function as seedbeds for the flowering of new supportive friendships. Such was the case with our Friday night Codenames Zoom gathering that began in the first months of the pandemic and continues now as an almost ritualized gathering. As we continued our meetings and our relationships evolved, we weren't reluctant to share concerning details about one's health. In my case, I didn't routinely offer an update on my condition, but it was difficult to avoid once it was on the table because one or more of the participants would ask at each subsequent virtual gathering: "How is it going?" "How are you doing?" or "What's new?" Even though six of the participants were physicians and two were RNs, these queries weren't sterile medical probes. Rather, they were asked out of caring, supportive concern we had developed for each other. And if my response to their questions was vague, everyone knew that Roberta would reliably elaborate and fill in the holes. Either way, everyone was aware and concerned about my condition.

Another anchored virtual group—my Friday morning meetings with a new set of colleagues—emerged in an organic way at the outset of the pandemic. And here we were, now more than five years later, with both anchored groups still meeting virtually on Friday mornings and evenings. It wasn't because we sometimes didn't have other things scheduled, even including going out to dinner or taking side trips with other group members. It was because we wanted to catch up with each other and see how things were going. We had become caring and emotionally supportive friends whose relationships now transcended the original anchored context.

I sometimes experienced another kind of interactional support that is anchored in a kind of transient encounter called a "fleeting relationship."[6] These one-time, temporally compressed interpersonal encounters evincing evidence of some emotional interdependence are common. Most of us probably recall such fleeting encounters—whether standing in line, riding on public transportation, or flying—in which we were the beneficiary or purveyor of supportive comments or gestures, such as my encounter with the fellow traveler who inquired about my eye patch and thanked me for my military service. While such encounters are often uplifting, the proffered support is generally too fleeting to have the carrying power of emotional support nested in long-term relationships with significant others or germinating in recurrent anchored relationships.

I was also the beneficiary of various forms of support anchored in the medical arena, that is, in anchored professionals. A host of physicians attended to my various conditions from the time I was originally diagnosed with two different cancers, followed by several skin cancers and the troublesome clinical trial side effects. During the clinical trial, I benefitted from an ongoing flow of reciprocal communication between the trial team and other specialists and me, underscoring not only their accessibility and responsiveness, but that my input mattered. Of these professionals, none was more central and supportive than the clinical trial team consisting of my CLL/SLL oncologist, her oncology nurse practitioner, and the clinical trial coordinator.

All the physicians and their teams provided detailed and accessible information about the condition they were treating, appeared to answer whatever questions we asked the best they could at the time, and exhibited considerable caring concern. Among the seemingly endless appointments and encounters, the following highlight the expression of such concern: the calming, hopeful manner in which my urologic oncologist walked us through our first postsurgical diagnostic and prognostic meeting; the rapid response of my CLL/SLL oncologist, who called me from a cab in

New York City on her way to a professional meeting, calmly assuring me a concern wasn't as troubling as I feared; the hour or so the head of hemotology spent with me on the evening I was admitted to the hospital for tumor lysis, patiently answering questions and explaining the protocol while I waited for a room assignment; the confident and comforting way in which my ophthalmologist prepped me in the waiting room for emergency surgery to reduce the painful mounting pressure in my left eye; the many times my dermatologist promptly responded to my inquiries about a festering or new skin condition; and the detailed but relaxed and encouraging way in which my cardiac electrophysiologist discussed my AFib and my upcoming surgical procedure through which a stroke-reducing device (a "Watchman") would be implanted in the opening of the appendage attached to the left atrium of my heart.

Not all appointments were as expressively caring; many were follow-up visits like blood tests and scans, which had a perfunctory character to them. The character of attention and support I received across the physicians and their teams also varied somewhat by their centrality to my overall situation. While Roberta and I did a good deal of grumbling about the iatrogenic side effects as they escalated, we had no gnawing complaints about the physicians and their teams who treated them. To the contrary, we often commented to each other after one of our appointments how fortunate we were to have this set of physicians overseeing my various conditions.

This accessible and interactive channel of communication also illustrates the second advantage of the trial: teamwork. The three trial team members coordinated and worked together to oversee and monitor my treatment, difficulties, and progress. Rarely was there an appointment when two of the three team members weren't present, and all three were often in the exam room working in tandem. On infusion days, for example, Roberta and I would usually arrive early in the morning to get my blood drawn, followed by a meeting with the team for review of my status and a clinical palpation exam before I proceeded to the infusion lab. They initially asked me about how I was doing: How was I feeling physically? Mentally, too? Was I still pursuing my exercise routines? Still swimming? How was it going? Was I still sexually intimate, and if so, how was that affected? And what about side effects? If there was a worsening side effect, or anything new, the coordinator would make sure to take note for possible inclusion or elaboration of the daunting list of side effects.

They didn't just ask *me* what was going on. They also wanted to hear from Roberta, given that she was with me throughout the entire journey. Following the discussion of some of my responses and Roberta's observations, the NP or oncologist, depending on who was present, would proceed with a hands-on assessment of my lymph nodes and spleen in order to assess whether there was growth, stasis, or shrinkage. And if both the oncologist and NP were present, they would compare their clinical observations and thoughts aloud, sharing them with both Roberta and me. While this coordinated teamwork might strike some clients as duplicative and unnecessary, we found it of considerable value. And what heightened its value was our involvement, which the trial team invited and clearly supported. I wasn't treated as an experimental, laboratory object. Rather, I was made to feel like an active agent in the diagnostic and treatment processes, as was Roberta.

It was this kind of patient empowerment that made a difference to us. We felt that what we had to say, what we offered, mattered. That itself was a source of considerable support, but of a different order than the more emotion-laden words usually associated with social support.

During my journey, one of my longtime good friends asked me several times if I found comforting support in religion. He was also curious whether I prayed, especially during the most trying times, as when I was initially diagnosed with two cancers and my thoughts turned to "circling the wagons" as I lay alone hospitalized late at night trying to come to grips with what had just transpired. My friend's curiosity made sense given his flirtation with the priesthood earlier in life and our frequent discussions of religion because he had audited a couple of seminars I taught on the sociology of religious movements.

I told him that I considered prayer on that first trying night in the hospital, and on several occasions afterward, such as when I woke up in 2022 completely blind in my left eye. But I didn't pray—even though the Gospel stories of Jesus restoring the vision of a number of blind men came to mind. In fact, I hadn't prayed for years, for myself or for others, but not because of some atheistic obstinance. Growing up in a churchgoing family, I recall praying some in childhood, less so in high school, and rarely in college, even though I considered pursuing an advanced degree in theology my senior year. But after my experience as a draftee in the army during the Vietnam War years, and my work as a clinical psychology technician in a mental hygiene clinic at a stateside base, I began to doubt the point and power of prayer. It wasn't that I discounted the link between stress and fear and a reach for spiritual reassurance, but there was little to no reference to that connection among the many combat vets I screened who had been on "search and destroy" missions and waded through the rice paddies of Vietnam. Rather, I was struck by the psychologically troubling and lingering consequences of their trying combat experiences.

From that point on I engaged in an ongoing tussle with the question of theodicy, of how a supposedly good and caring God could exist in a world plagued with war, violence, and all kinds of hateful discord. In addition, my late wife's long-term battle with cancer in the face of all the prayers I was told she received disabused me even more of its efficacy. So praying was now a distant and seemingly ineffectual ritual, especially when it involved intercessory prayers for the healing of others. Besides, I felt rather hypocritical to even think about engaging in a religious activity I had eschewed years ago.

With all that in mind, I told my friend that I didn't pray or engage regularly in any other form of ritualized religious activity aimed at activating the supportive intervention of a presumed higher power or mystical force. To note my reluctance to pray, however, is not to say that I saw no value in prayer or the support of those who are religiously inspired, as with another longtime friend who is a Catholic priest and walked with us the day of my initial surgeries and sat with Roberta the night of my emergency eye surgery. I also understood that prayer—and the kindred activities of chanting and meditation, both of which I had experimented with—can be of psychological value in reducing feelings of stress and increasing self-confidence. I also knew that I was somewhat of an outlier, as prayer, or some parallel religious ritual, is common worldwide, including among most Americans. According to a 2023–2024 nationwide survey of some thirty-six thousand adults, 44 percent said they pray every day, with another 23 percent saying they pray weekly or several times a month.[7] And most that do so believe that it not only makes a positive difference in their lives, but also in the lives of those for whom they pray.

I welcomed the prayers of others, not because I thought they might magically facilitate my healing, but because they constituted another form of emotional support.[8] For example, when I returned to the pool three weeks after my eye surgery, a fellow swimmer asked where I had been. I told him I was unable to swim for a while because of eye surgery, which prompted further inquiry and disclosure of my blinded left eye. He said, "I am so sorry, man! You'll be in my prayers." That stuck with me throughout my swim, and still does, because it reminded me that emotional support can be issued at unexpected times in different ways in different places. Hence, I welcomed such intercessory prayers, rather than discarded them, because they expressed, albeit in a religious vernacular, caring concern about my condition and well wishes for my recovery. As such, they were also a source of social support.

We all need some form of augmented social support at various junctures in our lives, and there are few times when that need is more essential than when experiencing serious illness or disability. Clichéd truisms, to be sure. But they were driven home again and again while I negotiated various cancers, COVID, and a clinical trial, along with its troublesome side effects, during the pandemic years. It wasn't that I hadn't understood the salience of social support as the principal caregiver for my late wife, Judy, during her bouts with cancer and eventual passing. But there was something about the lived experience of being a candidate for and recipient of social support in its various forms that sharpened my appreciation for its indispensability in dealing with the mercurial and challenging character of cancer and its treatment.

I find it difficult to imagine how I would have negotiated many of these challenges without the support of my significant others, particularly Roberta. I also came to appreciate that social support, particularly of the emotional and self-affirming variants, can be issued in various bounded, anchored contexts, whether in an exercise facility or virtual Zoom group, even if the supportive connections don't transcend the context. But sometimes they do, blossoming into new supportive friendships.

I also came to appreciate the nuanced ways in which some physicians and their teams, as with my clinical trial team, could provide supportive encouragement beyond tangible, physiological support. Also, I have come to value the prayers and chants of others in ways that I hadn't for years—not as healing balms but as expressions of concern and well-being in the vernacular of their religious base. And most generally, I have been struck how the diagnosis of cancer and participation in a clinical trial calls forth the caring concern and supportive goodwill of significant others, transituational and anchored friends and acquaintances, and even some physicians and their teams, together comprising a web of supportive social relationships that proved invaluable in navigating between the realms of living and simply existing.

CHAPTER 13

Between Living and Existing

The attributes of liminality or of liminal personae . . . are necessarily ambiguous, since this condition and these persons elude or slip through the network of classifications that normally locate states and persons in cultural space. Liminal entities are neither here nor there; they are betwixt and between.

—VICTOR TURNER[1]

In the first year of the pandemic, particularly those first months of shelter-in-place orders and social distancing, Roberta and I found ourselves watching too much TV, including the Netflix reality series *Queer Eye*. In the series, five guys with specialized skills in personal grooming, fashion, interior design, cooking and libations, and cultural currencies and trends work together to give lifestyle makeovers to selected people. One episode featured a restaurant owner on the outskirts of Austin, Texas, who was still grieving the death of his wife nearly ten years earlier. Their Cajun, crayfish-focused restaurant was in the same state of repair as it was when she passed, as was his appearance and life: same mullet hairdo, same weathered attire, and same despondent look. The *Queer Eye* team created a twofold plan: resuscitate the widower's life and renovate the restaurant in a style that would have put a smile on the late wife's face. At some point during the revitalization process, the grieving restaurant operator said, "It's too easy to exist and too hard to live."

That cautionary expression of the widower's liminal experience resonated with me on several fronts. When Judy passed away in April 2005, I found *myself* existing rather than living. Other than resuming my teaching obligations at the university and visiting my nearby children, I spent much of my time reminiscing about our lives together, trying to magically recapture, indeed relive, some of the special moments, and generally living in the past rather than moving forward. I spent several evenings each week sitting in my easy chair typing up memories and feelings on my laptop while nursing a good portion of a bottle of red wine with soft music in the background. Once a sense of catharsis surfaced, I would usually call it an evening. I spent too many evenings this way for the better part of six months. Grieving will do that, of course. But at some point, one has to work their way through the bewilderment of loss if they are to begin living again rather than simply existing.

My four siblings, our mother, my adult children, and a few friends helped to keep me afloat, functioning much like buoys in a choppy sea. But what really lifted the fog of grief was meeting Roberta in the fall of 2005. It was through her and our evolving relationship that I found myself living once again, which was pretty much a steady state for the next fifteen years. The COVID pandemic, the adverse development of my variant of lymphoma, and my resultant participation in the clinical trial and its sobering side effects changed all that. Their confluence, like the churning vortex at the intersection of three raging rivers, sometimes threatened to suck me back from the reclaimed life of living into the rut of simply existing again.

It was at these times when I was most likely to feel down in the dumps, bordering on the edge of depression but without sinking into it or slumping into a bout of anomic confusion about the seriousness and life-defining salience of my condition. In those moments, I would find myself on the verge of surrendering to the identity of a cancer victim and the treatment process in which I was engulfed. Of course, my web of supportive social relationships played a critical role in keeping me from sliding into and getting stuck in one of these ruts. But certain personal and biographic factors also made a difference.

One such factor was the force of habit and the determination to not let my constructive precancer habits wither. In addition to trying to maintain my precancer exercise routine of swimming, walking, and weightlifting, I continued my volunteer involvement with organizations dedicated to serving my community. I was a board member in two nonprofit organizations that provided services for local urban poor and homeless residents, on the board of another organization dedicated to peacemaking, and served on a task force appointed by the city council to address homelessness in our town. Like most organizations during the early days of the pandemic, these nonprofits conducted their meetings virtually on Zoom, which made it easier for most folks to participate in their organizations' respective meetings and stay engaged, at least virtually.

The virtual gatherings worked so efficiently and effectively in some contexts that they became the new normal for some purposes even after the pandemic subsided. Had the organizations with which I was associated returned fully to in-person meetings, it would have been difficult to maintain my participation. But fortunately, they continued with the Zoom meeting option. Even then, sometimes I needed to suspend my participation because I didn't feel up to it. This was especially the case during the run-up to the clinical trial, and then again during the trial. One of the nonprofits, for example, scheduled their meetings at seven thirty in the morning, which coincidentally usually followed an eight- to ten-hour infusion day. The resultant fatigue and periodic intestinal distress, coupled with the early morning time, often made participation too trying, both physically and mentally. Nonetheless, I would often give it a shot, sometimes prompting Roberta to ask, "Why stay on all the boards, given what you're going through?" My son asked a similar question when I was coediting a five-volume encyclopedia on social and political movements.

He'd say quizzically, "You have cancer and you're in a clinical trial. Why would you even bother?"

I usually muttered something about a sense of obligation and wanting to stay on top of things. "Besides, what else should I do?" I asked.

Such rationales were not off-base, but they were really secondary to a more pressing motivation: I didn't want to put my life on hold by suspending my previous routines, thereby raising the white flag of surrender. In other words, I was intent on resisting the pull of the cancer identity peg the best I could. The drive was to stay engaged, or at least try to do so, although not always successfully.

My sense is that while the tension between falling into the rut of existing rather than living is commonplace among cancer victims, I also suspect that many try to remain engaged as long as they can, even following a dire diagnosis and prognosis. Judy's experience is illustrative. In spring 2004, shortly after we learned that her breast cancer had metastasized in her brain and she initiated radiation therapy, she wanted to return to work as a medical librarian for six hours a day. Her radiation oncologist gave her the green light to do so, but with the proviso that someone else drive her to and from work. I agreed to do so and sequestered myself in the library to work on my laptop until she was ready to return home at the end of her workday. Her reengagement with work lasted only six weeks, however, as the radiation failed to control the tumors in her brain, and the cancer metastasized in the liver. I suppose I could have asked her why she insisted on returning to work. But I never did because I knew the answer. Returning to work not only provided a lever of hope, but it importantly gave her another focus of attention. Something else to think about other than her failing condition until she couldn't.

I saw this same motivational dynamic at play in other cancer victims as well. A close friend of Roberta's and mine was diagnosed with a rare kind of renal cancer around six months after completion of my clinical trial. Excision of the affected kidney appeared to remove the cancer, but several months later abdominal discomfort prompted another scan revealing metastasis. Escalating pain and a terminal prognosis followed. Targeted immunotherapy helped blunt the pain, but with other complications that paused and then halved the immunotherapy. Throughout all of this, as a semiretired physician he tried to maintain his patient commitments at a nearby medical center the best he could, and even resumed in a tempered fashion his two favorite pastimes: playing tennis and hiking. We and other friends also went hiking with him on a couple of occasions. But a few of our mutual friends found this somewhat baffling given his apparent terminal condition. I, however, wasn't surprised. Not only was he a compassionate and determined man, but his efforts were consistent with my experience and what I observed with my late wife and others. Just like them, he wasn't ready to throw in the towel.

The driving impulse, even when in death's driveway, is to reach for and grasp the foundational pilings of living, the defining cornerstones of one's precancerous life that have given it meaning and shaped its identity. That's what my late wife did, that's what our friend did, and that's what I tried to do. To hang on to those pilings is to remind oneself that being victimized by cancer doesn't mean you have to put your life completely on hold. To do otherwise is to risk falling into and staying mired in the rut of existing rather than living.

Staying in the realm of living is not easy, however. Not only are there the physical challenges that invariably come with cancer and its treatment, any of which can throw you off course. As I experienced during the clinical trial, for a stretch of time I would feel like I had reclaimed the markers of living, only to be pushed back into the rut of existence with a new debilitating side effect. I also found the nagging psychological challenges often even more difficult to negotiate than the physiological ones. Even when I was in the realm of living, I never felt as if I was fully encapsulated within it. Rather, there was a feeling of marginality, as if I were living in a gray zone of uncertainty, initially anxiously anticipating activation of the cancer when in the watch-and-wait status or anticipating its reoccurrence when in remission. I don't think I ever felt ownership of the realm of living. Rather, I felt more like a renter subject to eviction by factors beyond my control. I thus came to realize that the realms of living and existing are not binaries but endpoints of a continuum in which one is likely to be skewed in one direction or another throughout the journey. In other words, the experience of being situated in this liminal state, fluctuating between the cancer-free realm of living and the cancer-impacted realm of existing struck me as a kind of "new normal" that would define my life going forward.

The concept of new normal describes a previously unfamiliar set of activities that have become increasingly customary in lieu of the former routinized activities that have been disrupted and put on hold. The phrase became more common in the wake of the COVID pandemic and came to encompass such activities as work from home, Zooming, lockdown and quarantine, and wearing face masks. The concept also gained some currency in oncology, referring to "the changes a person faces as a result of cancer and its treatments," and the "adjustments cancer survivors make as they define what will be their new normal."[2]

There is, however, a fundamental difference between the new normal regimen of activities triggered by the pandemic or other disruptions of daily life and those sparked by the onset of cancer and its treatment. Many of the new normal activities elicited by the pandemic, such as mask wearing and fist-bumping, began to wither, in part because of the public's tiring of these cautionary measures and also because of the decreasing severity of infections due to the significant protective effects of vaccination. The new normal associated with the occurrence of cancer and its treatment persists, on the other hand, because of cancer's devious and mercurial character and the unpredictable adverse effects of its treatment regimens. At the same time, I realized that staying close to what was previously normal, what I thought of as the realm of living, was contingent on hanging onto the pilings and moorings of that realm. Otherwise, I would have let cancer define my being and found myself simply existing rather than living. This was an ongoing challenge, of course, not only because of cancer's capricious physiological nature, but also because of its colonization of my consciousness.

CHAPTER 14

Does the Cancer Odyssey Ever Really End?

My advice to other disabled people would be, concentrate on things your disability doesn't prevent you doing well, and don't regret the things it interferes with. Don't be disabled in spirit as well as physically.

—STEPHEN HAWKING[1]

On a glorious coastal Southern California morning in April 2024, the sun was in full bloom, the sky clear ocean blue except for scattered, distant cirrus clouds, the temperature a pleasant seventy to seventy-two. A soft ocean breeze cooled the beads of sweat dripping down my face on the last leg of my three-mile walk, which I'd interspersed with fifteen minutes of machine-aided weightlifting about ten minutes earlier. I paced myself to the beat of pop tunes I had downloaded over the years. As I listened to Fleetwood Mac's "Dreams," with a rush of exercise-induced endorphins now flowing through me, I felt almost euphoric.

And why not? I thought. *Here I am, exercising as I did almost seven years ago before the jarring revelation from an emergency room physician that I had two cancers. Sure, my pace, whether swimming or walking, is not as brisk as before, but I'm still doing it, the constraints of increasing age notwithstanding. What's more, I am in full remission, now exactly a full year and a half since completion of the clinical trial and learning that there was no measurable residual disease in the end-of-trial excised bone marrow specimen.*

Since then, I have had quarterly appointments with my oncologist, all preceded by blood draws, plus an annual CT scan of the neck, chest, abdomen, and pelvis, per the ten-year clinical trial protocols. My most recent appointment and set of exams showed continued complete remission. The test used in the detection and diagnosis of blood and bone marrow diseases reported "no immunophenotypic evidence of non-Hodgkin B cell lymphoma" in an assessment of ten thousand blood cells. And the CT scan showed continued shrinkage of the lymph nodes in my abdomen, with all now being close to the average non-lymphadenopathy node size or smaller. And my odds for continued progression-free survival looked good in light of recent research comparing four treatment regimens, which found that among the patients in the venetoclax–obinutuzumab–ibrutinib group, 92.2 percent had no detectable minimal residual disease at fifteen months, with three-year progression-free survival at 90.5 percent, which were the highest rates of undetectable minimal residual disease (uMRD) among the four regimens.[2]

A few weeks after the positive appointment with my oncologist, I had my first cystoscopy in six months. Here, too, the exam was upbeat. Since the bladder looked healthy with no signs of distress, the oncology urologist suggested that we move from a six-month schedule to an annual one. That change was clearly good news to Roberta and me, since for the better part of the past seven years I had been on a quarterly schedule with a cystoscopy every three months. This past year was the exception as we moved to a six-month schedule. Now, with a normal-looking bladder except for the scar from the initial excised tumor, I was pleased to know that I wouldn't have to schedule a cystoscopy for more than once a year.

My clinical trial–triggered irregular heartbeat, the AFib, is still with me although under control. And the markedly increased risk it poses for strokes has been reduced by the Watchman device that was threaded through my femoral vein and implanted in the opening to the left atrial appendage of my heart, several months after the clinical trial ended. It is in that appendage that most stroke-inducing blood clots are formed, so implanting the little parachute-like device reduces the probability of an AFib-generated stroke by about 90 percent, according to the electrophysiologist who did the intravenous surgery. In addition, the Watchman reduces the need to be on the level of anticoagulants recommended for most people with AFib, and further reduced the small chance of a bleed in my remaining eye or elsewhere. Another reason for feeling good.

And my latest appointment with my dermatologist also delivered good news: only one precancerous lesion requiring just a squirt of neutralizing frozen liquid nitrogen. What a contrast to the half dozen or so suspicious lesions that routinely caught his attention during previous visits, with a number requiring Mohs surgery, including excision of a small portion of my right ear coupled with six weeks of radiation. But he found nothing suspicious this time except for the one small lesion.

"Your skin looks better than I've ever seen it," he said with surprise.

"Maybe that's not so surprising," I said, "since I've been wearing a rash guard shirt for some time now when swimming."

Probably more important than that, I suggested, was that I might well be less prone to skin cancers since I'd completed the clinical trial and had been in remission for a year and a half, thus reminding him that I was no longer prone to the increased risk of developing skin cancer from CLL/SLL. "Maybe that's it," he responded. Whatever the explanation for my lesion-free skin this time, the exam outcome added to the reasons for feeling good.

But this stream of upbeat feelings was tempered by my impaired vision. Short of some miraculous advance in research on vision restoration or eye transplants, my blinded left eye will remain a functionally useless ride-along for the rest of my life. I still haven't figured out what having only one functioning eye means in terms of my sightedness. Am I 50 percent sighted or blind, or somewhere in between? With only one eye and limited depth perception, I am clearly a person with significant vision loss, and thus visually impaired. The National Federation of the Blind says there are "no generally accepted definitions" for these and other visual statuses such as low vision. Even the overlap of definitions of blindness, among the National Federation of the Blind and the American Community Survey of disabilities, for example, is rather untidy.[3] But does the absence of such consensually agreed-upon diagnostic categories really matter? As Andrew Leland notes in his memoir at the end of sight due to retinitis pigmentosa, "Vision is a powerfully subjective substance, one that is still most accurately measured by the patient's own report."[4]

For me, then, assessment of my impaired vision hinges on its functionality. What difference does it make, or has it made, in terms of the quality of my life? My experience is that it is not so much the quality of life that has changed as its character. My impaired sight hasn't significantly changed what I can do with but a few exceptions requiring optimal depth perception, such as playing Ping-Pong, badminton, tennis, and pool, which for me were infrequent activities anyway; rather, it has made me more conscious, more aware of how I do whatever I am doing. The "doing" of everyday life customarily becomes habituated for all of us, but much of what I previously took for granted has now become problematic. It's not that I can't do most of what I previously did; it's that the doing of those routine everyday things has changed. And it's a change to which I am still adjusting, and one that is often a source of frustration and simmering anger, as Roberta sometimes reminds me.

Even more disquieting, the impaired sightedness is an ever-present reminder of cancer and the clinical trial. Metaphorically, it is an everyday ride-along that can't be pushed out the door. There are moments, however, when the right mixture of feeling-good, flying-high feelings override consciousness of such pestering ride-alongs, such as during my walk on that beautiful April morning. But such euphoric moments are experientially episodic and fleeting. And even if they were more recurrent and enduring, my experience is that they are subject to fracture by the fickle nature of cancer and the discomforting messaging often associated with it and its treatment. Illustrative was the message I received from my urologist's office two weeks after my most recent cystoscopy indicating that my urine cytology revealed "some atypical cells" and that I was to have another urine test to "evaluate the etiology of the atypical cells." This had happened twice before on the heels of a cystoscopy, but with no concerning results, so I wasn't too worried about the possible revelation of trace elements of cancer in my urine. But the notification and scheduling of another urine test to check out the atypical cells was still a jolt of the kind that yanked concern about cancer from the backstage of consciousness to the front stage. Once again, for a while anyway, it was back on my mind.

And if such unanticipated messages aren't unsettling enough, being reminded that uMRD could still mean cancer cells are lurking in the blood or bone marrow is almost certain to tarnish the shine on the word remission. "Undetectable minimal residual disease only means that cancer cells haven't been detected," as a long-term CLL survivor, who has been in and out of remission several times, discouragingly reminded me on one occasion. As clearly explained in a CLL website article on measurable residual disease:

Unfortunately, uMRD does not imply a cure. Since CLL and SLL are chronic, slow-growing cancers, relapse still occurs. However, uMRD is associated with a deeper remission and a longer progression-free survival time, compared to those who have detectable MRD. It is still necessary to monitor the disease and watch for symptoms to help detect when the cancer is returning.[5]

It's why the CLL and Leukemia & Lymphoma Society websites remind us that even when we're in complete remission, we should be on the lookout for available treatment options should the cancer resurface.

Such is the uncertain nature of the cancer odyssey. And that is why concern about its reemergence lingers in the backstage of consciousness, readily pulled to the forefront by emergent physiological agitations, a series of new tests, watch-and-wait messaging, and reminders to keep your antenna up for new treatment regimens.

"Was the clinical trial worth it?" I have been asked on numerous occasions. The answer is an easy one: It was worth it, unquestionably! I am in complete remission, hopefully for the remainder of my life, which may have been shortened had it not been for the clinical trial. I have a couple of noxious trial side effects—the AFib and blinded left eye—that will travel with me for the rest of my life, to be sure. None of this has derailed my life. I can still travel and negotiate daily life in a way that I was unable to do before the trial, albeit with some compensatory modifications, and thus I try to live rather than simply exist.

Indeed, cancer, much like my impaired sightedness, has expanded and deepened my awareness, indeed my consciousness, and my appreciation of the nuances of my everyday surrounds and life, particularly of the importance of family and friends. Even though I now see the world with only one eye, I see many things more clearly than before.

In an unexpected and ironic way, aspects of my life have been enriched, even though the cancer odyssey, unlike Odysseus's, is probably never-ending.

An Odyssey Coda

The historically transcendent appeal and durability of classical myths—like Homer's epic poems *The Iliad* and *The Odyssey*—reside in two defining features. First, they speak to the timeless trials and tribulations of living coursing through the human experience across the ages, providing stories for understanding and giving meaning to those experiences, whether in relation to birth, love, family, home, loss and grief, victory or defeat, or other culturally shared challenges. In the words of the late Joseph Campbell, one of the foremost authorities on mythology, "Myth helps you to put your mind in touch with this experience of being alive. It tells you what the experience is,"[1] or at least provides a frame for situating and interpreting it. And second, the mythic stories and their themes are polyvalent in that they can be drawn on and applied in almost limitless ways to illuminate the difficult problems and challenges experienced across the human experience. Because of this wide-ranging interpretive utility, myths are almost infinitely resonant, thus rendering somewhat pointless questions and debate as to whether they are being interpreted correctly, such as "What is *The Odyssey*'s most important point or lesson?" The answer, it seems, depends on how the mythic story as a whole, or parts of it, resonate with the experience(s) in question.

For me, there is no single book or challenging encounter in *The Odyssey* that captures the entirety of my journey navigating several overlapping cancers, a clinical trial and its adverse side effects, and a forty-five-day encounter with COVID in the midst of the pandemic. A number of Odysseus's challenges function as touchstones for illuminating an aspect of my odyssey, such as the reference to the Sirens' cry as a metaphor for the waxing and waning of cancer consciousness. And the encounter with Polyphemus, the Cyclops who Odysseus cunningly tricks and blinds, enabling his escape with his men, could be used metaphorically to capture the muting of the cancer via the clinical trial regimen of targeted therapies. But far more significant and resonant for me, as well as for most cancer victims I suspect, is the general theme running through all of *The Odyssey*'s books and obstacles: the importance of determination and resilience in the face of adversity and surmounting the challenges thrown one's way, and full-throated engagement with life and one's significant others throughout the journey and beyond, however much time we have.

Odyssey Medical Timeline

2017

Oct. 8: Gross hematuria

Oct. 9: Emergency room dual diagnosis of bladder cancer and lymphoma; hospitalized for observation, further diagnostics, and prep for surgery

Oct. 12: Surgical excision of bladder tumor and of large underarm lymph node

Oct. 13: Released from hospital with preliminary lymphoma diagnosis of CLL/SLL

Oct. 26: Diagnostic appointment with oncology urologist and referral to CLL oncologist

Nov.: Initial meeting with CLL oncologist; reviewed diagnosis and informed of "watch and wait" status

2018

SLL still dormant; remained in watch-and-wait status

2019

Jul 1: Retired, in part due to increasing fatigue and some intestinal issues, but still in watch-and-wait status

2020

Jan. 31: World Health Organization (WHO) and US Department of Health and Human Services declare COVID-19 as an emergency

Mar. 11: WHO declares a pandemic

Mar. 19: California Governor Gavin Newsom issues the country's first statewide stay at home order

Apr. 14: Drove to university hospital ER at 4:00 a.m. Easter Sunday for severe abdominal pain diagnosed as diverticulosis

June 4: Mohs surgery for lesion on tragus of right ear with meta-static potential called pleomorphic dermal sarcoma; tragus removed

July: Drenching night sweats for about four weeks

Aug. 17: Transurethral resection of two malignant bladder polyps with blue light cystoscopy and cysview

Aug.-Sep.: Six weeks (thirty sessions) of radiation therapy for suspected pleomorphic dermal sarcoma

2021

Winter-Spring: Cancer progression; SLL no longer dormant

July 26: Initiation of fifteen-month clinical trial with first dose of ibru-tinib and loading dose of Cazyva via infusion

July 28: Hospitalized for three days and nights with significant tumor lysis syndrome

Oct. 26: Hospitalized overnight for venetoclax ramp-up from 10 to 50 mgs to guard against another episode of tumor lysis syndrome

Dec. 25: Omicron COVID-19 variant now the dominant strain, account-ing for more than 70 percent of US cases according to CDC

Dec. 28: Tested positive for COVID-19 (Omicron variant) with home antigen test

Dec. 29: PCR confirmed the positive antigen test result

Dec. 30: Received sotrovimab monoclonal antibody infusion for treatment of COVID-19 because of high risk for progression to severe COVID due to being immunocompromised

2022

Jan. 24-Feb. 10: Ibrutinib and venetoclax suspended due to prolonged COVID

Feb. 10: Negative COVID test, finally, forty-five days later

Feb. 15: Received two Evusheld shots, one in each buttock (Evusheld is a new monoclonal antibody to provide preventive protection from COVID-19 in patients who are immunocompromised and may not gain much protection from vaccines.)

Feb. 25: Diagnosed with atrial fibrillation and put on Eliquis

Mar. 28: Sixth and final obinutuzumab infusion, which had been suspended a number of times because of low platelet counts and COVID

Mar. 31: Platelet count registered 35, lowest since beginning the clinical trial; trial drugs and Eliquis suspended in order to elevate the platelet count

Apr. 14: Platelet count rising over the last two weeks, reaching 90 today; although still below the 150 cutoff for low normal, the ibrutinib and venetoclax regimen is resumed

Apr. 21: Sudden change in vision in left eye

May 16: Diagnosed with retinal hemorrhage in left eye; told the hemorrhage should self-correct

June 13: No improvement or self-correction in left eye; began a series of retinal injections to keep the vision loss from worsening and to staunch the bleeding

June 30: Outpatient cardioversion with transesophageal echocardiogram; in normal sinus rhythm for only a day and a half, then back into AFib

Aug. 15: Appointment with opthamologist; retinal injections discontinued because treatment wasn't retarding the retinal bleeding; impaired vision was now chronic and probably immutable; functionally, no central vision because of the hemorrhage, but do have peripheral vision and light penetration

Sep. 1: Met with cardiologist (electrophysiologist) to discuss options for dealing with my AFib (he recommended surgical insertion of the Watchman device rather than an ablation.)

Sep. 6: Awakened with no vision in left eye; completely blind eye

Sep. 7: Because of continued bleeding in left eye, ibrutinib discontinued and Eliquis halted

Sep. 19: Surgery to remove blood and blood clots from hemorrhaging left eye and to reduce eye pressure and associated pain, but with no change in impaired vision

Oct. 13: Final day of fifteen-month clinical trial with blood work, pre-hydration infusion followed by three contrast-based CT scans for neck, chest, and abdoment, and the posthydration infusion, followed by bone marrow biopsy

Nov. 3: Appointment with oncologist for posttrial assessment; bone marrow biopsy found no detectable residual cancer cells (uMRD), and CT scan showed normalizing lymph nodes; in complete remission with good prognosis

2023

Jan. 19: Surgical insertion of Watchman into left atrial appendage to reduce prospect of blood clot-induces strokes; hospitalized for night for monitoring

2024

Feb. 15: Ongoing trial quarterly follow-up with oncologist; abdominal CT scan showed lymph nodes of normal size, and flow cytometry of blood draw found "no evidence (uMRD) of non-Hodgkin B cell lymphoma"; remain in remission with favorable prognosis
Oct. 28: Diagnosed with wet macular degeneration in the functional right eye, and initiation of monthly retinal injections to stop its progression

2025

August: Remain in remission with favorable prognosis, but still receiving retinal injections in the right eye to control the wet macular degeneration and maintain the eye's functionality as optimally as possible

Acknowledgments

Just as cancer survival is contingent on the depth and breadth of one's social support, so the authorship of a book about one's journey negotiating cancer is affected by the kinds of support received from others. Indeed, it is arguable that rarely, if ever, is a book authored by a solo author, even if the book cover says otherwise. And this is especially so, I suspect, for books authored by those who have negotiated and recovered from a serious illness. This certainly holds for me, as there are numerous others to whom I am indebted for their encouragement to write this book, for their willingness to read it and provide constructive feedback, or for doing both.

Foremost among those who have been a source of inspirational encouragement and helpful feedback is my wife, Roberta. As detailed throughout the book, she was by my side as a loving caregiver, as a fellow observer providing another set of eyes and ears, and as an editorial muse. If this were a curtain call, Roberta would be center stage with me.

Also on stage, but in the shadows, would be my late wife, Judy, whose role would be akin to a mnemonic muse, reminding me of her long and life-ending experience with cancer. That is the role she played in relation to the authorship of this book as well. Her ordeal and our journey together, with me as her principal caregiver, were baked into my memory and thus colored my experiences and interpretation of cancer and its treatment. Clearly, the book would have been written differently had it not been for Judy's cancer odyssey and my memory of it at critical junctures throughout my journey.

My siblings—particularly my two sisters, Roberta and Deborah, and my middle brother, Randy, and their spouses, Barbara and Leslee—read every word of every chapter in the first draft, and provided helpful and encouraging feedback, which was accented by Roberta's and Leslee's former careers as RNs. Roberta also shared the manuscript with a number of her friends who were negotiating cancer personally or as a caregiver for a spouse, all of whom found the manuscript resonant and provided encouraging feedback.

Among my friends who read the entire manuscript, or a portion of it, I am particularly indebted to Jevelyn, who read and commented on every initial chapter, not only from the perspective of a physician with expertise in internal medicine, but also from the vantage point of a cancer survivor. I am also deeply indebted to my late close friend Larry, who passed away suddenly a few days after calling to check on me and provide some feedback on the most recent chapter I had sent for his review. That marked the twelfth chapter he had read, after which he would call to share his thoughts, which were always candid but encouraging. Thanks as well to Leon, Richard, and Katarin, three fellow sociologists and friends, and Iris, a creative friend of Roberta's, and three of her former students—Izzy, a doctoral student in public health; Samantha, then a fourth year medical student; and DJ, an internal medicine resident at the time—for reading all or a portion of the manuscript.

I am also appreciative of a number of other friends and colleagues who were wellsprings of encouragement in their own way. They include Alan, David, Doug, James, John, Junling, Pat, Rafael, Steve, Walter, Willie, Yang, and Jon, an internationally renowned interventional cardiologist and organizer of the Friday night Zoom group who passed away due to renal cancer just prior to the completion of this book.

I didn't ask my three middle-aged children to read the book as it evolved, in large part because I didn't want to bother them given their busy lives. But knowing they were there was a source of encouragement, for which I am most thankful.

I also extend my gratitude to the CLL Society for being a veritable font of information on CLL/SLL and for its various support groups, one of which I attended quite regularly on a monthly basis.

As well, I would like to acknowledge and thank the various physicians who attended to me throughout my odyssey and who were thus important contributors to the book. They are noted throughout by their medical specialty, but not by name in order to ensure their anonymity.

Finally, thanks to my substantive editor, Abigail, for her enthusiastic engagement with the manuscript and her constructive suggestions, and to the Greenleaf Book Group team, especially Dee, Trinity, and Adrianna, for their assistance in advancing the book through the publication process.

Notes

Preface

1. Neil J. Smelser, *The Odyssey Experience: Physical, Social, Psychological, and Spiritual Journeys* (University of California Press, 2009).

2. Kenneth Miller et al., "Use of the Word 'Cure' in Oncology," *Journal of Oncology Practice* 9, no. 4 (2013): 136–140, https://pmc.ncbi.nlm.nih.gov/articles/PMC3710180/pdf/jope136.pdf.

Introduction

1. Susan Sontag, *Illness as a Metaphor and AIDS and Its Metaphors* (Picador, 1990), 3.

2. For a broader discussion of authoethnographies, see Leon Anderson, "Analytic Autoethnography," *Journal of Contemporary Ethnography* 35, no. 4 (2006): 373–395, https://doi.org/10.1177/0891241605280449; and Arthur P. Bochner and Carolyn Ellis, *Evocative Autoethnography: Writing Lives and Telling Stories* (Routledge, 2016). I consider this book a blend of these two approaches to autoethnography—analytic and evocative—but with a slight skew toward the evocative approach.

3. On spousal grief, see Deborah Carr and John Shep Jeffreys, "Spousal Bereavement in Later Life," in *Grief and Bereavement in Contemporary Society: Bridging Research and Practice*, eds. Robert A. Neimeyer et al. (Routledge/Taylor & Francis, 2011), 81–92, https://sites.bu.edu/deborah-carr/files/2018/01/carrjeffreys_2011.pdf.

4. C. Wright Mills, *The Sociological Imagination*, 40th anniversary edition (Oxford University Press, 2000).

5. According to the National Cancer Institute's Division of Cancer Control and Population Studies, there are eighteen million-plus cancer survivors as of January 2022, with an estimated increase of eight million by 2040. See Emily Tonorezos et al., "Prevalence of Cancer Survivors in the United States," *Journal of the National Cancer Institute* 116, no. 11 (2024): 1784–1790, https://doi.org/10.1093/jnci/djae135.

6. Michael Stein, *The Lonely Patient: How We Experience Illness* (Harper Perennial, 2007), 10.

7. Siddhartha Mukherjee, *The Emperor of All Maladies: A Biography of Cancer* (Scribner, 2010).

Chapter 1

1. For an overview of depression as clinically defined, see "Depression," National Institute of Mental Health, 2023, https://www.nimh.nih.gov/health/topics/depression.

2. Dean Mobbs et al., "On the Nature of Fear," *Scientific American*, October 10, 2019, https://www.scientificamerican.com/article/on-the-nature-of-fear/#.

3. Harvard School of Public Health, "Great Public Desire to Seek Early Diagnosis of Alzheimer's," *Science Daily*, July 20, 2011, https://www.sciencedaily.com/releases/2011/07/110720115300.htm.

4. Nicole M. Else-Quest and Tracy L. Jackson, "Cancer Stigma," in *The Stigma of Disease and Disability: Understanding Causes and Overcoming Injustices*, ed. Patrick W. Corrigan (American Psychological Association, 2014), 166. See also Catherine E. Mosher and Sharon Danoff-Berg, "Death Anxiety and Cancer-Related Stigma: A Terror Management Analysis," *Death Studies* 31, no. 10 (2007): 885–907.

5. Illustrative of the increased survival rate, for example, is the 29.2 percent decline in US death rates for all types of cancer from 1999 to the present, with an even larger percentage decrease (43.3) for non-Hodgkin lymphoma. See "U.S. Cancer Statistics: Data Visualizations," Centers for Disease Control and Prevention and National Cancer Institute, 2024, https://www.cdc.gov/cancer/dataviz.

6. Barney G. Glaser and Anselm L. Strauss, *Awareness of Dying* (Aldine, 1965).

Chapter 2

1. Christal Pollock, "The Canary in the Coal Mine," *Journal of Avian Medicine and Surgery* 30, no. 4 (2016): 386–391.

2. For conceptualization of relief and discussion of its different types, see A. J. Graham et al., "Relief in Everyday Life," *Emotion* 23, no. 7 (2023): 1844–1868, https://doi.org/10.1037/emo0001191; Eva M. Krockow, "Is There More Than One Type of Relief?," *Psychology Today*, March 23, 2021, https://www.psychologytoday.com/us/blog/stretching-theory/202103/is-there-more-one-type-relief?eml.

3. Stein, *The Lonely Patient*, 8-9.

4. See Charles Horton Cooley, *Human Nature and the Social Order* (Charles Scribner's Sons, 1902).

5. For discussion of the relationship between the roles we play and our identities, and identity salience and its determinants, see Sheldon Stryker, *Symbolic Interactionism: A Social Structural Version* (Benjamin-Cummings, 1980; repr., Blackburn Press, 2002); Jan E. Stets and Richard T. Serpe, "Identity Theory," in *Handbook of Social Psychology*, eds. John DeLamater and Amanda Ward (Springer, Dordrecht, 2013), 31–60, https://doi.org/10.1007/978-94-007-6772-0_2.

6. See David Snow and Leon Anderson, "Identity Work Among the Homeless: The Verbal Construction and Avowal of Personal Identities," *American Journal of Sociology* 92, no. 6 (1987): 1336–1371, DOI:10.1086/228668.

7. Tumor markers are identified through a procedure called immunophenotyping. See Scott D. Boyd et al., "Selective Immunophenotyping for Diagnosis of B-cell Neoplasms: Immunohistochemistry and Flow Cytometry Strategies and Results," *Applied Immunohistochemistry Molecular Morphology* 21, no. 2 (2013): 116–31, DOI:10.1097/PAI.0b013e31825d550a.

8. Siddhartha Mukherjee, *The Song of the Cell: An Exploration of Medicine and the New Human* (Scribner, 2022), 350.

9. The rate at which cancer cells are increasing is measured principally through the Ki-67 (a protein found in dividing cells) proliferation index. For discussion, see "Ki-67 Proliferation Index," National Cancer Institute, https://www.cancer.gov/publications/dictionaries/cancer-terms/def/ki-67-proliferation-index; "What Is the Ki-67 Proliferation Index?," *Biology Insights*, August 4, 2025, https://biologyinsights.com/what-is-the-ki-67-proliferation-index/; Qin Liang et al., "Effect of Ki-67 Expression Levels and Histological Grade on Breast Cancer Early Relapse in Patients with Different Immunohistochemical-based Subtypes," *Scientific Reports* 10, no. 7648 (2020), https://doi.org/10.1038/s41598-020-64523-1.

10. "Watch and Wait (Active Observation)," CLL Society, https://cllsociety.org/cll-sll-patient-education-toolkit/watch-and-wait-active-observation/.

Chapter 3

1. For discussion of consciousness and the relationship between emotions and feelings, see Antonio Damasio, *The Feeling of What Happens: Body and Emotion in the Making of Consciousness* (Harcourt, 1999).

2. For an overview of the similarities and differences of B cells and T cells in the context of the immune system, see Devon Carter, "T Cells, B Cells and the Immune System," M. D. Anderson Cancer Center, November 10, 2021, https://www.mdanderson.org/cancerwise/t-cells--b-cells-and-the-immune-system.h00-159465579.html. See also Mukherjee's discussions of B and T cells in *The Song of the Cell*.

3. "Cancer Stat Facts: Non-Hodgkin Lymphoma," National Cancer Institute, 2025, https://seer.cancer.gov/statfacts/html/nhl.html. For estimated new cases and deaths for common cancer types in 2025, see "Cancer Stat Facts: Common Cancer Sites," National Cancer Institute, 2025, https://seer.cancer.gov/statfacts/html/common.html.

4. For basic information and statistics on non-Hodgkin lymphoma, see: "Non-Hodgkin Lymphoma (Adults)," American Cancer Society, https://www.cancer.org/cancer/types/non-hodgkin-lymphoma.html

5. Mukherjee, *The Song of the Cell*, 186-201.

6. Kathryn Rizzo and Mehdi Nassiri, "Diagnostic Workup of Small B Cell Lymphomas: A Laboratory Perspective," *Lymphoma* (2012), https://doi.org/10.1155/2012/346084.

7. For a compilation and discussion of these diagnostic enigmas, see Lisa Sanders, *Every Patient Tells a Story: Medical Mysteries and the Art of Diagnosis* (Broadway Books/Random House, 2009).

8. Danielle Ofri, "Falling into the Diagnostic Trap," *New York Times*, July 19, 2012, https://danielleofri.com/falling-into-the-diagnostic-trap/.

9. For an elaborated discussion of anomie both structurally and individually, see Robert K. Merton, *Social Theory and Social Structure*, chapters VI and VII (Free Press, 1968).

10. Rahul Jandial, *This Is Why You Dream: What Your Sleeping Brain Reveals About Your Waking Life* (Penguin Life, 2024).

Chapter 4

1. Albert Camus, *The Plague* (Modern Library, 1948; repr., Vintage International, 1991), 36–37.

2. COVID-19 is the abbreviation for Coronavirus Disease 2019, which is more technically known as severe acute respiratory syndrome coronavirus 2 (SARS-CoV-2). For a timeline of key data points and public health and political decisions during the pandemic in the US and worldwide, see "CDC Museum COVID-19 Timeline," Centers for Disease Control and Prevention, https://www.cdc.gov/museum/timeline/COVID19.html/.

3. For discussion of the roots of this divisiveness, see Doug McAdam and Karina Kloos, *Deeply Divided: Racial Politics and Social Movements in Postwar America* (Oxford University Press, 2014).

4. For a discussion of the anti-vaccination movement, see Kevin A. Estep and David A. Snow, "Anti-Vaccination Movement and Science Denialism," in *Contemporary Social Movements: Descriptive and Historical Accounts*, eds. David A. Snow, Doug McAdam, and D. A. Moss (Wiley Blackwell, 2026), 184-190.

5. For analysis of the politicization of COVID mitigation initiatives, see: David A. Snow, "COVID-19 Pandemic, Collective Behavior, and Protest," in *The Wiley Blackwell Encyclopedia of Social and Political Movements*, 2nd ed., eds., David. A. Snow et al. (Wiley Blackwell, 2023), 511–516. See also, Donatella della Porta, "COVID-19 Pandemic and Social Movements" in *The Wiley Blackwell Encyclopedia of Social and Political Movements*, 2nd ed., eds., David. A. Snow et al. (Wiley Blackwell, 2023), 516–525.

6. Sean C. Mueller et al., "Changes in Ultrafine Particle Concentrations Near a Major Airport Following Reduced Transportation Activity During the COVID-19 Pandemic," *Environmental Science & Technology Letters* 9, no. 9 (2022): 706–711, https://doi.org/10.1021/acs.estlett.2c00322/.

7. Adie Tomer and Lara Fishbane, "Coronavirus Has Shown Us a World Without Traffic. Can We Sustain It?," Brookings Metro, May 1, 2020, https://www.brookings.edu/research/coronavirus-has-shown-us-a-world -without-traffic-can-we-sustain-it/.

8. Jesse Matheson, "How Has Coronavirus Affected Pubs, Cafes, and Restaurants?" Economics Observatory, July 2, 2020, https://www .economicsobservatory.com/how-has-coronavirus-affected-pubs-cafes -and-restaurants/.

9. Andre Chu Qiao Lo et al., "Case of Pleomorphic Dermal Sarcoma with Systematic Review of Disease Characteristics, Outcomes, and Management," *BMJ Case Reports* 14, no. 8 (2021), https://casereports.bmj .com/content/14/8/e244522.

10. Jeremy Yuen-Chun Teoh et al., "Recurrence Mechanisms of Non-Muscle-Invasive Bladder Cancer—A Clinical Perspective," *Nature Reviews Urology* 19 (2022): 280–294, https://doi.org/10.1038/s41585-022-00578-1.

11. N. David Yanez et al., "COVID-19 Mortality Risk for Older Men and Women," *BMC Public Health* 20, no. 1742 (2020), https://doi. org/10.1186/s12889-020-09826-8.

Chapter 5

1. Mukherjee, *The Emperor of All Maladies*, 577.

Notes

2. William Piersol, "Does Exercise Improve Survival After a Cancer Diagnosis? An Encouraging New Study," Memorial Sloan Kettering Cancer Center, September 15, 2023, https://www.mskcc.org/news/does-exercise-improve-survival-after-cancer-diagnosis-encouraging-new-study; Jessica A. Lavery et al., "Pan-Cancer Analysis of Postdiagnosis Exercise and Mortality," *Journal of Clinical Oncology* 41, no. 32 (2023): 4982–4992, https://ascopubs.org/doi/pdf/10.1200/JCO.23.00058?role=tab.

3. Peter Titlebaum, "Rebranding Watch and Wait," CLL Society, February 26, 2025, https://cllsociety.org/2025/02/rebranding-watch-and-wait/.

4. Brian Koffman, "What Is a Lymph Node?," CLL Society, March 15, 2016, https://cllsociety.org/2016/03/what-is-a-lymph-node/.

5. Mark É. Czeisler et al., "Delay or Avoidance of Medical Care Because of COVID-19–Related Concerns—United States, June 2020," *Morbidity and Mortality Weekly Report* 69, no. 36 (2020): 1250–1257, http://dx.doi.org/10.15585/mmwr.mm6936a4.

6. For a more extensive discussion of these factors, see Joseph D. Tariman et al., "Physician, Patient, and Contextual Factors Affecting Treatment Decisions in Older Patients with Cancer and Models of Decision Making: A Literature Review," *Oncology Nursing Forum* 39, no. 1 (2012): E70–83, https://doi:10.1188/12.ONF.E70-E83.

7. John C. Byrd et al., "Targeting BTK with Ibrutinib in Relapsed Chronic Lymphocytic Leukemia," *New England Journal of Medicine* 369, no. 1 (2013): 32–42, https://DOI:10.1056/NEJMoa1215637.

8. "IMBRUVICA® (Ibrutinib) Approved by U.S. FDA for the First-line Treatment of Chronic Lymphocytic Leukemia," PR Newswire, March 4, 2016, https://www.prnewswire.com/news-releases/imbruvica-ibrutinib-approved-by-us-fda-for-the-first-line-treatment-of-chronic-lymphocytic-leukemia-300231107.html.

9. For discussion of BTK in B cell cancer, see Simar Pal Singh et al., "Role of Bruton's Tyrosine Kinase in B cells and Malignancies," *Molecular Cancer* 17, no. 57 (2018), .https://doi.org/10.1186/s12943-018-0779-z.

10. Koffman, "What Is a Lymph Node?"

11. Nathan Vardi, *For Blood and Money: Billionaires, Biotech, and the Quest for a Blockbuster Drug* (W.W. Norton, 2023), 79.

12. Vardi, *For Blood and Money*, 142.

13. Vardi, *For Blood and Money*, 142.

14. *Oncology* staff, "BTK Inhibition and Treatment Options in Chronic Lymphocytic Leukemia," *ONCOLOGY Companion* 37, no. 3 (2023): 23–27, https://www.cancernetwork.com/view/recap-btk-inhibition-and-treatment-options-in-chronic-lymphocytic-leukemia.

15. See, for example: Kirsten Fischer et al., "Venetoclax and Obinutuzumab in Patients with CLL and Coexisting Conditions," *New England Journal of Medicine* 380, no. 23 (2019): 2225–2236, https://DOI:10.1056/NEJMoa1815281

16. Mamta Sachdeva and Sameer Dhingra, "Obinutuzumab: A FDA Approved Monoclonal Antibody in the Treatment of Untreated Chronic Lymphocytic Leukemia," *International Journal of Applied & Basic Medical Research* 5, no. 1 (2015): 54–57, https://doi.org/10.4103/2229-516X.149245.

17. Mukherjee, *The Song of the Cell*, 200.

18. Keith Loria, "Up, Up and Not Going Away: Cancer Drug Prices," *Managed Healthcare Executive* 32, no. 10 (2022): 70–72. https://www.managedhealthcareexecutive.com/view/up-up-and-not-going-away-cancer-drug-prices. See also Loren Collado and Isaac Brownell, "The Crippling Financial Toxicity of Cancer in the United States," *Cancer Biology & Therapy* 20, no. 10 (2019): 1301–1303, https://DOI:10.1080/15384047.2019.1632132; and Vardi, *For Blood and Money*, 150, 153.

Chapter 6

1. Louis Schneider, *The Sociological Way of Looking at the World* (McGraw-Hill, 1975).

2. Ann Liu, "ASH 2021: Dr. Jennifer Woyach on a Clinical Trial in Progress with Combination Ibrutinib, Venetoclax, and Obinutuzumab," CLL Society, June 2, 2022, https://cllsociety.org/2022/06/

ash-2021-dr-jennifer-woyach-on-a-clinical-trial-in-progress-with-combination-ibrutinib-venetoclax-and-obinutuzumab/.

3. Angeliki Tsiouris et al., "What Is the Image of the 'Typical Cancer Patient?' The View of Physicians," *American Journal of Men's Health* 15, no. 2 (2021): 1–11. https://journals.sagepub.com/doi/10.1177/1557988320988480.

4. The concept iatrogenesis and its analytic utility for thinking about things gone wrong in the course of medical care and treatment caught my attention when rereading former colleague Louis Schneider's *The Sociological Way of Looking at the World*, which articulates its overlap with the sociological concept of unintended consequences.

5. Atul Gawande, *Complications: A Surgeon's Notes on an Imperfect Science* (Henry Holt, 2002), 56.

6. Andrea Goethals et al., "Femoral Hernia," *StatPearls [Internet]*, May 3, 2025, https://www.ncbi.nlm.nih.gov/books/NBK535449/.

7. Mukherjee, *The Emperor of All Maladies*.

8. Arjun Gupta and Joseph A. Moore, "Tumor Lysis Syndrome," *JAMA Oncology* 4, no. 6 (2018): 895, https://doi:10.1001/jamaoncol.2018.0613.

Chapter 7

1. These and related COVID figures come from the David J. Sencer CDC Museum COVID-19 Timeline, which runs from late-2019 into mid-2022. See "CDC Museum COVID-19 Timeline," Centers for Disease Control and Prevention, https://www.cdc.gov/museum/timeline/COVID19.html.

2. Stacey Adjei et al., "Mortality Risk Among Patients Hospitalized Primarily for COVID-19 During the Omicron and Delta Variant Pandemic Periods—United States, April 2020–2022," *Morbidity and Mortality Weekly Report* 71, no. 37 (2022): 1188, doi: 10.15585/mmwr.mm7137a4; Betzaida Tejada-Vera and Ellen A. Kramarow, "COVID-19 Mortality in Adults Aged 65 and Over: United States, 2020," *NCHS Data Brief* 446 (2022), DOI: https://dx.doi.org/10.15620/cdc:121320; and N. David

Yanez et al., "COVID-19 Mortality Risk for Older Men and Women,"
BMC Public Health 20, no. 1742 (2020), https://doi.org/10.1186/
s12889-020-09826-8.

3.   For discussion of how the PCR test works, see Nimrat Khehra et al.,
"Polymerase Chain Reaction (PCR)," *StatPearls [Internet]*, updated July 7,
2025, https://www.ncbi.nlm.nih.gov/books/NBK589663/.

4.   National Library of Medicine, "Access to Healthcare and Disparities in
Access," in *2021 National Healthcare Quality and Disparities Report* (Agency
for Healthcare Research and Quality, 2021), https://www.ncbi.nlm.nih.
gov/books/NBK578537/.

5.   These COVID figures come from the David J. Sencer CDC Museum
COVID-19 Timeline, which runs from late-2019 into mid-2022.
"CDC Museum COVID-19 Timeline," Centers for Disease Control and
Prevention, https://www.cdc.gov/museum/timeline/COVID19.html.

6.   Jandial, *This Is Why You Dream*, 189.

7.   Julia Landwehr, "Why Even a Faint Line on Your COVID Test Still Means
You're Positive," *Health*, updated November 29, 2024, https://www.health.
com/news/faint-line-COVID-test.

8.   Emily Alpert Reyes, "This Treatment Can Protect Vulnerable People
from COVID. But Many Don't Know About It," *Los Angeles Times*,
March 6, 2022, https://www.latimes.com/california/story/2022-03-06/
COVID-antibody-treatment-obstacles.

Chapter 8

1.   Mayo Clinic Staff, "Atrial Fibrillation: Symptoms, Causes," Mayo Clinic,
https://www.mayoclinic.org/diseases-conditions/atrial-fibrillation/
symptoms-causes/syc-20350624.

2.   Jonathan W. Friedberg, "Vitamin D and Lymphoma: An
Apparent Benefit, but Further Study Required," *The ASCO Post*,
April 25, 2020, https://ascopost.com/issues/april-25-2020/
vitamin-d-and-lymphoma-an-apparent-benefit-but-further-study-required/.

3. Intermountain Medical Center, "New Study Links Excessive Amounts of Vitamin D to Onset of Atrial Fibrillation," EurekAlert!, November 16, 2011, https://www.eurekalert.org/news-releases/804716; and Lana Barhum, "Vitamin D Overdose Symptoms You Shouldn't Ignore," Verywell Health, October 30, 2024, https://www.verywellhealth.com/symptoms-of-too-much-vitamin-d-8736991.

4. Mayo Clinic Staff, "Vitamin D," Mayo Clinic, March 21, 2025, https://www.mayoclinic.org/drugs-supplements-vitamin-d/art-20363792.

5. Kathy Charmaz, *Good Days, Bad Days: The Self in Chronic Illness and Time* (Rutgers Press, 1991).

6. "Low Vision and Legal Blindness Terms and Descriptions," American Foundation for the Blind, 2024, https://www.afb.org/blindness-and-low-vision/eye-conditions/low-vision-and-legal-blindness-terms-and-descriptions.

Chapter 9

1. For discussion of the relationship between visual impairment and balance, see Byoung-Jin Jeon and Tae-Hyun Cha, "The Effects of Balance of Low Vision Patients on Activities of Daily Living," *Journal of Physical Therapy Science* 25, no. 6 (2013): 693–696, https://www.jstage.jst.go.jp/article/jpts/25/6/25_jpts-2013-004/article.

2. Stein, *The Lonely Patient*, 121.

Chapter 10

1. Elisabeth Kübler-Ross, *On Death and Dying* (Scribner, 1969).

2. See Andra Cătălina Roşca et al., "Psychological Consequences in Patients With Amputation of a Limb. An Interpretative-Phenomenological Analysis," *Frontiers in Psychology* (2021), doi: 10.3389/fpsyg.2021.537493. PMID: 34122200; PMCID: PMC8189153.

Chapter 11

1. Mukherjee, *The Song of the Cell*, 352-353.

2. The concept was originally coined and elaborated by sociologist Talcott Parsons. See Talcott Parsons, *The Social System* (Routledge, 1951). For critical discussions and extensions of the concept, see Nanna Mik-Meyer and Anne Roelsgaard Oblong, "The Negotiation of the Sick Role: General Practitioners' Classification of Patients with Medically Unexplained Symptoms," *Sociology of Health & Illness* 34, no. 7 (2012): 1025–1038, https://doi.org/10.1111/j.1467-9566.2011.01448.x; Martin I Standal et al., "Health, Work, and Family Strain – Psychosocial Experiences at the Early Stages of Long-Term Sickness Absence," *Frontiers in Psychology* 12 (2021), https://doi.org/10.3389/fpsyg.2021.596073; Matthias Zick Varul, "Talcott Parsons, the Sick Role and Chronic Illness," *Body & Society* 16, no. 2 (2010): 72–94, https://doi.org/10.1177/1357034X10364766.

Chapter 12

1. For an overview of research, see Peggy A. Thoits, "Mechanisms Linking Social Ties and Support to Physical and Mental Health," *Journal of Health and Social Behavior* 52, no. 2 (2011): 145–161, doi: 10.1177/00221465510395592; Debra Umberson and Jennifer Karas Montes, "Social Relationships and Health: A Flashpoint for Health Policy," *Journal of Health and Social Behavior* 51, suppl. (2010): S54–S66, doi: 10.1177/00221465510383501.

2. Jane D. McLeod et al., "Health Inequalities," in *Handbook of the Social Psychology of Inequality*, Jane D. McLeod et al., eds. (Springer, 2014): 715–742.

3. Daniel A. Cox, "The State of American Friendship: Change, Challenges, and Loss," Survey Center on American Life, June 8, 2021, https://www.americansurveycenter.org/research/the-state-of-american-friendship-change-challenges-and-loss/; and Isabel Goddard, "What Does Friendship Look Like in America?" Pew Research Center, October 12, 2023, https://pewrsr.ch/3tlzqsr.

4. Cox, "The State of American Friendship."

5. For a broader discussion of anchored personal relationships in relation to personal relationships as usually understood, see Calvin Morrill et al., eds., *Together Alone: Personal Relationships in Public Places* (University of California Press, 2005), 16–18.

6. For discussion of fleeting relationships and how they differ from anchored relationships, see Morrill et al., *Together Alone.*

7. "Religious Landscape Study," Pew Research Center, 2025, doi: 10.58094/3zs9-jc14.

8. For a summary discussion of the ways in which prayer does and doesn't work, see Phil Zuckerman, "Does Prayer Work? Yes and No," *Psychology Today*, September 30, 2019, https://www.psychologytoday.com/us/blog/the-secular-life/201909/does-prayer-work. See also Benedict Carey, "Long–Awaited Medical Study Questions the Power of Prayer," *The New York Times*, March 31, 2006, https://www.nytimes.com/2006/03/31/health/longawaited-medical-study-questions-the-power-of-prayer.html.

Chapter 13

1. Victor Turner, *The Ritual Process: Structure and Anti-Structure* (Aldine, 1969), 95.

2. Deborah Christensen, "How Will You Define Your New Normal?," ONS/VOICE, September 24, 2020, https://voice.ons.org/news-and-views/how-will-you-define-your-new-normal#; "Life After Cancer Treatment," National Cancer Institute, updated April 1, 2025, https://www.cancer.gov/about-cancer/coping/survivorship/new-normal.

Chapter 14

1. Claudia Dreifus, "Conversation with Stephen Hawking: Life and the Cosmos, Word by Painstaking Word," *New York Times*, May 11, 2011, https://www.nytimes.com/2011/05/10/science/10hawking.html.

2. B. Eichhorst et al., "First-Line Venetoclax Combinations in Chronic Lymphocytic Leukemia," *The New England Journal of Medicine* 388,

no. 19 (2023): 1739–1754, https://www.nejm.org/doi/pdf/10.1056/
NEJMoa2213093.

3. "Blindness Statistics," National Federation of the Blind, 2019, https://nfb.
org/resources/blindness-statistics#; and "Disability Statistics," ILR Yang-
Tan Institute on Employment and Disability Cornell University. 2025.
https://www.ilr.cornell.edu/yti/work/disability-statistics.

4. Andrew Leland, *The Country of the Blind: A Memoir at the End of Sight*
(Penguin, 2023), 53.

5. See also "Measurable Residual Disease (MRD)," CLL Society, 2025,
https://cllsociety.org/cll-sll-patient-education-toolkit/measurable-residual-
disease-mrd/ and Shenmiao Yang et al., "Is Unmeasurable Residual Disease
(uMRD) the *Best* Surrogate Endpoint for Clinical Trials, Regulatory
Approvals and Therapy Decisions in Chronic Lymphocytic Leukemia
(CLL)?" *Leukemia* 36 (2022): 2743–2747, https://doi.org/10.1038/
s41375-022-01699-7.

An Odyssey Coda

1. Joseph Campbell with Bill Moyers, *The Power of Myth* (Doubleday, 1988), 6.

Bibliography

Adjei, Stacey, Kai Hong, Noelle-Angelique M. Molinari et. al. "Mortality Risk Among Patients Hospitalized Primarily for COVID-19 the Omicron and Delta Variant Pandemic Periods—United States, April 2020–2022." *Morbidity and Mortality Weekly Report* 71, no. 37 (2022): 1182–1189. doi: 10.15585/mmwr.mm7137a4.

American Cancer Society. "Non-Hodgkin Lymphoma (Adults)." https://www.cancer.org/cancer/types/non-hodgkin-lymphoma.html.

American Foundation for the Blind. "Low Vision and Legal Blindness Terms and Descriptions." 2024. https://www.afb.org/blindness-and-low-vision/eye-conditions/low-vision and-legal-blindness-terms-and-descriptions.

Anderson, Leon. "Analytic Autoethnography." *Journal of Contemporary Ethnography* 35, no. 4 (2006): 373–395. https://doi.org/10.1177/0891241605280449.

Barhum, Lana. "Vitamin D Overdose Symptoms You Shouldn't Ignore." Verywell Health, October 30, 2024. https://www.verywellhealth.com/symptoms-of-too-much-vitamin-d-8736991.

Biology Insights. "What Is the Ki-67 Proliferation Index?" August 4, 2025. https://biologyinsights.com/what-is-the-ki-67-proliferation-index/.

Bochner, Arthur P. and Carolyn Ellis. *Evocative Autoethnography: Writing Lives and Telling Stories* (Routledge, 2016).

Boyd, Scott D., Yasodha Natkunam, John R. Allen, and Roger R. Warnke. "Selective Immunophenotyping for Diagnosis of B-cell Neoplasms: Immunohistochemistry and Flow Cytometry Strategies and Results." *Applied Immunohistochemistry Molecular Morphology* 21, no. 2 (2013): 116–131. https://DOI:10.1097/PAI.0b013e31825d550a.

Byrd, John C., Richard R. Furman, Steven E. Coutre et al. "Targeting BTK with Ibrutinib in Relapsed Chronic Lymphocytic Leukemia." *New England Journal of Medicine* 369, no. 1 (2013): 32–42. https://DOI:10.1056/NEJMoa1215637.

Campbell, Joseph with Bill Moyers. *The Power of Myth*. Doubleday, 1988.

Camus, Albert. *The Plague.* Modern Library, 1948. Reprint, First Vintage International, 1991.

Carey, Benedict. "Long–Awaited Medical Study Questions the Power of Prayer." *The New York Times.* March 31, 2006. https://www.nytimes.com/2006/03/31/health/longawaited-medical-study-questions-the-power-of-prayer.html.

Carr, Deborah and John Shep Jeffreys. "Spousal Bereavement in Later Life." In *Grief and Bereavement in Contemporary Society: Bridging Research and Practice*, edited by Robert A. Neimeyer, Darcy L. Harris, Howard R. Winokuer, and Gordon F. Thornton. (Routledge/Taylor & Francis, 2011).

Carter, Devon. "T Cells, B Cells and the Immune System." M. D. Anderson Cancer Center. November 10, 2021. https://www.mdanderson.org/cancerwise/t-cells--b-cells-and-the-immune-system.h00-159465579.html.

Centers for Disease Control and Prevention. "CDC Museum COVID-19 Timeline." https://www.cdc.gov/museum/timeline/COVID19.html.

Centers for Disease Control and Prevention and National Cancer Institute. "US Cancer Statistics: Data Visualizations." 2024. https://www.cdc.gov/cancer/dataviz.

Charmaz, Kathy. *Good Days, Bad Days: The Self in Chronic Illness and Time.* Rutgers Press, 1991.

Christensen, Deborah. "How Will You Define Your New Normal?" ONS VOICE. September 24, 2020. https://voice.ons.org/news-and-views/how-will-you-define-your-new-normal#.

CLL Society. "Measurable Residual Disease (MRD)." 2025. https://cllsociety.org/cll-sll-patient-education-toolkit/measurable-residual-disease-mrd/.

CLL Society. "Watch and Wait (Active Observation)." https://cllsociety.org/cll-sll-patient-education-toolkit/watch-and-wait-active-observation/.

Collado, Loren and Isaac Brownell. "The Crippling Financial Toxicity of Cancer in the United States." *Cancer Biology & Therapy* 20, no. 10 (2019): 1301–1303. https://DOI:10.1080/15384047.2019.1632132.

Cooley, Charles Horton. *Human Nature and the Social Order.* Charles Scribner's Sons, 1902.

Cox, Daniel A. "The State of American Friendship: Change, Challenges, and Loss." Survey Center on American Life, June 8, 2021. https://www.americansurveycenter.org/research/the-state-of-american-friendship-change-challenges-and-loss/.

Czeisler, Mark É., Kristy Marynak, Kristie E. N. Clarke et al. "Delay or Avoidance of Medical Care Because of COVID-19–Related Concerns—United States, June 2020." *Morbidity and Mortality Weekly Report* 69, no. 36 (2020): 1250–1257. http://dx.doi.org/10.15585/mmwr.mm6936a4.

Damasio, Antonio. *The Feeling of What Happens: Body and Emotion in the Making of Consciousness.* Harcourt, 1999.

della Porta, Donatella, "COVID-19 Pandemic and Social Movements." *The Wiley Blackwell Encyclopedia of Social and Political Movements*, 2nd ed., edited by David A. Snow, Donatella della Porta, Doug McAdam, and Bert Klandermans, (Wiley Blackwell, 2023), 516-525.

Dreifus, Claudia. "Conversation with Stephen Hawking: Life and the Cosmos, Word by Painstaking Word." *The New York Times*, May 11, 2011. https://www.nytimes.com/2011/05/10/science/10hawking.html.

Eichhorst, B., C. U. Niemann, A. P. Kater, M. Fürstenau et al. "First-Line Venetoclax Combinations in Chronic Lymphocytic Leukemia." *New England Journal of Medicine* 388, no. 19 (2023): 1739–1754. https://www.nejm.org/doi/pdf/10.1056/NEJMoa2213093.

Else-Quest, Nicole M. and Tracy L. Jackson. "Cancer Stigma." In *The Stigma of Disease and Disability: Understanding Causes and Overcoming Injustices*, edited by Patrick W. Corrigan (American Psychological Association, 2014). 165–181.

Estep, Kevin A. and David A. Snow, "Anti-Vaccination Movement and Science Denialism," *Contemporary Social Movements: Descriptive and Historical Accounts*, edited by David A. Snow, Doug McAdam, and Dana A. Moss. (Wiley Blackwell, 2026). 184-190.

Fischer, Kirsten, Othman Al-Sawaf, Jasmin Bahlo et al. "Venetoclax and Obinutuzumab in Patients with CLL and Coexisting Conditions." *New England Journal of Medicine* 380, no. 23 (2019): 2225–2236. https://DOI:10.1056/NEJMoa1815281.

Friedberg, Jonathan W. "Vitamin D and Lymphoma: An Apparent Benefit, but Further Study Required." *The ASCO Post*, April 25, 2020. https://ascopost.com/issues/april-25-2020/vitamin-d-and-lymphoma-an-apparent-benefit-but-further-study-required/.

Gawande, Atul. *Complications: A Surgeon's Notes on an Imperfect Science*. Henry Holt, 2002.

Glaser, Barney G. and Anselm L. Strauss. *Awareness of Dying*. Aldine, 1965.

Goddard, Isabel. "What Does Friendship Look Like in America?" Pew Research Center, October 12, 2023. https://pewrsr.ch/3tlzqsr.

Goethals, Andrea, Chaudhary Ehtsham Azmat, Parth J. Patel, and Curtis T. Adams. "Femoral Hernia." *StatPearls [Internet]*. May 3, 2025. https://www.ncbi.nlm.nih.gov/books/NBK535449/.

Graham, A. J., T. McCormack, S. Lorimer et al. 2022. "Relief in Everyday Life." *Emotion* 23, no. 7 (2023): 1844–1868. https://doi.org/10.1037/emo0001191.

Gupta, Arjun and Joseph A. Moore. "Tumor Lysis Syndrome." *JAMA Oncology* 4, no. 6 (2018): 895. https://doi:10.1001/jamaoncol.2018.0613.

Harvard School of Public Health. "Great Public Desire to Seek Early Diagnosis of Alzheimer's." Science Daily. July 20, 2011. https://www.hsph.harvard.edu/news/press-releases/alzheimers-international-survey/.

ILR Yang-Tan Institute on Employment and Disability, Cornell University. "Disability Statistics." 2025. https://www.ilr.cornell.edu/yti/work/disability-statistics.

"IMBRUVICA® (Ibrutinib) Approved by U.S. FDA for the First-line Treatment of Chronic Lymphocytic Leukemia." PR Newswire. March 4, 2016. https://www. prnewswire.com/news-releases/imbruvica-ibrutinib-approved-by-us-fda-for-the-first-line-treatment-of-chronic-lymphocytic-leukemia-300231107.html.

Intermountain Medical Center. "New Study Links Excessive Amounts of Vitamin D to Onset of Atrial Fibrillation." EurekAlert!, November 16, 2011. https://www. eurekalert.org/news-releases/804716.

Jandial, Rahul. *This Is Why You Dream: What Your Sleeping Brain Reveals About Your Waking Life*. Penguin Life, 2024.

Jeon, Byoung-Jin and Tae-Hyun Cha. "The Effects of Balance of Low Vision Patients on Activities of Daily Living." *Journal of Physical Therapy Science* 25, no. 6 (2013): 693–696. https://www.jstage.jst.go.jp/article/jpts/25/6/25_jpts-2013-004/_article.

Khehra, Nimrat, Inderbir S. Padda, and Muhammad Zubair. "Polymerase Chain Reaction (PCR)." *StatPearls [Internet]*. Updated July 7, 2025. https://www.ncbi.nlm. nih.gov/books/NBK589663/.

Krockow, Eva M. "Is There More Than One Type of Relief?" *Psychology Today*. March 23, 2021. https://www.psychologytoday.com/us/blog/stretching-theory/202103/ is-there-more-one-type-relief?eml.

Kübler-Ross, Elisabeth. *On Death and Dying*. Scribner, 1969.

Landwehr, Julia. "Why Even a Faint Line on Your COVID Test Still Means You're Positive." *Health*, updated November 29, 2024. https://www.health.com/news/ faint-line-COVID-test.

Lavery, Jessica A., Paul C. Boutros, Jessica M. Scott et al. "Pan-Cancer Analysis of Postdiagnosis Exercise and Mortality." *Journal of Clinical Oncology* 41, no. 32 (2023): 4982–4992. https://ascopubs.org/doi/pdf/10.1200/JCO.23.00058?role=tab.

Leland, Andrew. *The Country of the Blind: A Memoir at the End of Sight*. Penguin, 2023.

Liang, Qin, Ding Ma, Run-Fang Gao, and Ke-Da Yu. "Effect of Ki-67 Expression Levels and Histological Grade on Breast Cancer Early Relapse in Patients with Different Immunohistochemical-based Subtypes." *Scientific Reports* 10, no. 7648 (2020). https://doi.org/10.1038/s41598-020-64523-1.

Liu, Ann. "ASH 2021: Dr. Jennifer Woyach on a Clinical Trial in Progress with Combination Ibrutinib, Venetoclax, and Obinutuzumab." CLL Society, June 2, 2022. https://cllsociety.org/2022/06/ash-2021-dr-jennifer-woyach-on-a-clinical-trial-in-progress-with-combination-ibrutinib-venetoclax-and-obinutuzumab/.

Lo, Andre Chu Qiao, Sarah McDonald, and Kai Yuen Wong, "Case of Pleomorphic Dermal Sarcoma with Systematic Review of Disease Characteristics, Outcomes, and Management." *BMJ Case Reports* 14, no. 8 (2021). http://dx.doi.org/10.1136/bcr-2021-244522.

Loria, Keith. "Up, Up and Not Going Away: Cancer Drug Prices." *Managed Healthcare Executive* 32, no. 10 (2022): 70–72. https://www.managedhealthcareexecutive.com/view/up-up-and-not-going-away-cancer-drug-prices.

Matheson, Jesse. "How Has Coronavirus Affected Pubs, Cafes, and Restaurants?" Economics Observatory, July 2, 2020. https://www.economicsobservatory.com/how-has-coronavirus-affected-pubs-cafes-and-restaurants.

Mayo Clinic Staff. "Atrial Fibrillation: Symptoms, Causes." Mayo Clinic. https://www.mayoclinic.org/diseases-conditions/atrial-fibrillation/symptoms-causes/syc-20350624.

Mayo Clinic Staff. "Vitamin D." Mayo Clinic, March 21, 2025. https://www.mayoclinic.org/drugs-supplements-vitamin-d/art-20363792.

McAdam, Doug and Karina Kloos. *Deeply Divided: Racial Politics and Social Movements in Postwar America.* Oxford University Press, 2014.

McLeod, Jane D., Christy Erving, and Jennifer Caputo. "Health Inequalities." In *Handbook of the Social Psychology of Inequality*, edited by Jane D. McLeod, Edward J. Lawler, and Michael Schwalbe. Springer, 2014.

Merton, Robert K. *Social Theory and Social Structure.* Free Press, 1968.

Mik-Meyer, Nanna and Anne Roelsgaard Oblong. "The Negotiation of the Sick Role: General Practitioners' Classification of Patients with Medically Unexplained Symptoms." *Sociology of Health & Illness* 34, no. 7 (2012): 1025–1038. https://doi.org/10.1111/j.1467-9566.2011.01448.x.

Miller, Kenneth, Joseph H. Abraham, Lori Rhodes, and Rachel Roberts. "Use of the Word 'Cure' in Oncology." *Journal of Oncology Practice* 9, no. 4 (2013): 136–140. https://www.ncbi.nlm.nih.gov/pmc/articles/PMC3710180/pdf/jope136.pdf

Mills, C. Wright. *The Sociological Imagination*, 40th anniversary edition, with an afterword by Todd Gitlin. Oxford University Press, 2000.

Mobbs, Dean, Ralph Adolphs, Michael S. Fanselow et al. "On the Nature of Fear." *Scientific American*, October 10, 2019. https://www.scientificamerican.com/article/on-the-nature-of-fear/#.

Morrill, Calvin, David A. Snow, and Cindy White, editors. *Together Alone: Personal Relationships in Public Places.* University of California Press, 2005.

Mosher, Catherine E. and Sharon Danoff-Berg. "Death Anxiety and Cancer-Related Stigma: A Terror Management Analysis." *Death Studies* 31, no. 10 (2007): 885–907.

Mueller, Sean C, Neelakshi Hudda, Jonathan I. Levy et al., "Changes in Ultrafine Particle Concentrations Near a Major Airport Following Reduced Transportation Activity During the COVID-19 Pandemic." *Environmental Science & Technology Letters* 9, no. 9: 706–711. https://doi.org/10.1021/acs.estlett.2c00322/.

Mukherjee, Siddhartha. *The Emperor of All Maladies: A Biography of Cancer.* Scribner, 2010.

Mukherjee, Siddhartha. *The Song of the Cell: An Exploration of Medicine and the New Human.* Scribner, 2022.

National Cancer Institute. "Cancer Stat Facts: Common Cancer Sites." 2025. https://seer.cancer.gov/statfacts/html/common.html.

National Cancer Institute. "Cancer Stat Facts: Non-Hodgkin Lymphoma." 2025. https://seer.cancer.gov/statfacts/html/nhl.html.

National Cancer Institute. "Ki-67 Proliferation Index." https://www.cancer.gov/publications/dictionaries/cancer-terms/def/ki-67-proliferation-index.

National Cancer Institute. "Life After Cancer Treatment." April 1, 2025. https://www.cancer.gov/about-cancer/coping/survivorship/new-normal.

National Federation of the Blind. "Blindness Statistics." 2019. https://nfb.org/resources/blindness-statistics#.

National Institute of Mental Health. "Depression." 2023. https://www.nimh.nih.gov/health/topics/depression.

National Library of Medicine. "Access to Healthcare and Disparities in Access." In *2021 National Healthcare Quality and Disparities Report.* Agency for Healthcare Research and Quality, 2021. https://www.ncbi.nlm.nih.gov/books/NBK578537/.

Ofri, Danielle. "Falling into the Diagnostic Trap." *The New York Times*, July 19, 2012. https://danielleofri.com/falling-into-the-diagnostic-trap/.

ONCOLOGY staff. "BTK Inhibition and Treatment Options in Chronic Lymphocytic Leukemia." *ONCOLOGY Companion* 37, no. 3 (2023): 23–27. https://www.cancernetwork.com/view/recap-btk-inhibition-and-treatment-options-in-chronic-lymphocytic-leukemia.

Pal Singh, Simar, Floris Dammeijer, and Rudi W. Hendriks. "Role of Bruton's Tyrosine Kinase in B cells and Malignancies." *Molecular Cancer* 17, no. 57 (2018). https://doi.org/10.1186/s12943-018-0779-z.

Parsons, Talcott. *The Social System.* Routledge, 1951.

Pew Research Center. "Religious Landscape Study." 2025. doi: 10.58094/3zs9-jc14.

Piersol, William. "Does Exercise Improve Survival After a Cancer Diagnosis? An Encouraging New Study." Memorial Sloan Kettering Cancer Center. September 15, 2023. https://www.mskcc.org/news/does-exercise-improve-survival-after-cancer-diagnosis-encouraging-new-study.

Pollock, Christal. "The Canary in the Coal Mine." *Journal of Avian Medicine and Surgery* 30, no 4 (2016): 386–391.

Reyes, Emily Alpert. "This Treatment Can Protect Vulnerable People from COVID. But Many Don't Know About It." *Los Angeles Times*, March 6, 2022. https://www.latimes.com/california/story/2022-03-06/COVID-antibody-treatment-obstacles.

Rizzo, Kathryn and Mehdi Nassiri. "Diagnostic Workup of Small B Cell Lymphomas: A Laboratory Perspective." *Lymphoma* (2012). https://www.hindawi.com/journals/lymph/2012/346084/.

Roşca, Andra Cătălina, Cosmin Constantin Baciu, Vlad Burtăverde, and Alexandru Mateizer. "Psychological Consequences in Patients with Amputation of a Limb. An Interpretative-Phenomenological Analysis." *Frontiers in Psychology* (2021). doi: 10.3389/fpsyg.2021.537493. PMID: 34122200; PMCID: PMC8189153.

Sachdeva, Mamta and Sameer Dhingra. "Obinutuzumab: A FDA Approved Monoclonal Antibody in the Treatment of Untreated Chronic Lymphocytic Leukemia." *International Journal of Applied & Basic Medical Research* 5, no. 1 (2015): 54–57. https://doi.org/10.4103/2229-516X.149245.

Sanders, Lisa. *Every Patient Tells a Story: Medical Mysteries and the Art of Diagnosis.* Broadway Books/Random House, 2009.

Schneider, Louis. *The Sociological Way of Looking at the World.* McGraw-Hill, 1975.

Smelser, Neil J. *The Odyssey Experience: Physical, Social, Psychological, and Spiritual Journeys.* University of California Press, 2009.

Snow, David A. "COVID-19 Pandemic, Collective Behavior, and Protest." In *The Wiley Blackwell Encyclopedia of Social and Political Movements*, 2nd edition, edited by David A. Snow, Donatella della Porta, Doug McAdam, and Bert Klandermans. Wiley, 2023. 511–516.

Snow, David and Leon Anderson. "Identity Work Among the Homeless: The Verbal Construction and Avowal of Personal Identities." *American Journal of Sociology* 92, no. 6 (1987): 1336–1371. DOI:10.1086/228668.

Sontag, Susan. *Illness as a Metaphor and AIDS and Its Metaphors.* Picador, 1990.

Standal, Martin I., Vegard S. Foldal, Roger Hagen et al. "Health, Work, and Family Strain – Psychosocial Experiences at the Early Stages of Long-Term Sickness Absence." *Frontiers in Psychology* 12 (2021). https://doi.org/10.3389/fpsyg.2021.596073.

Stein, Michael. *The Lonely Patient: How We Experience Illness.* Harper Perennial, 2007.

Stets, Jan E. and Richard T. Serpe. "Identity Theory." In *Handbook of Social Psychology*, edited by John DeLamater and Amanda Ward. Springer, Dordrecht, 2013. https://doi.org/10.1007/978-94-007-6772-0_2.

Stryker, Sheldon. *Symbolic Interactionism: A Social Structural Version.* Benjamin-Cummings, 1980. Reprint, Blackburn Press, 2002.

Tariman, Joseph, Donna L. Berry, Barbara B. Cochrane, Ardith Z. Doorenbos, and Karen G. Schepp. "Physician, Patient, and Contextual Factors Affecting Treatment Decisions in Older Patients with Cancer and Models of Decision Making: A Literature Review." *Oncology Nursing Forum* 39, no. 1 (2012): E70–83. https://doi: 10.1188/12.ONF.E70-E83. PMID: 22201670.

Tejada-Vera, Betzaida and Ellen A. Kramarow. "COVID-19 Mortality in Adults Aged 65 and Over: United States, 2020." *NCHS Data Brief* 446 (2022). DOI: https://dx.doi.org/10.15620/cdc:121320.

Teoh, Jeremy Yuen-Chun, Ashish M. Kamat, Peter C. Black, et al. "Recurrence Mechanisms of Non-Muscle-Invasive Bladder Cancer—A Clinical Perspective." *Nature Reviews Urology* 19 (2022): 280–294. https://doi.org/10.1038/s41585-022-00578-1.

Thoits, Peggy A. "Mechanisms Linking Social Ties and Support to Physical and Mental Health." *Journal of Health and Social Behavior* 52, no. 2 (2011): 145–161. doi: 10.1177/0022146510395592.

Titlebaum, Peter. "Rebranding Watch and Wait." CLL Society, February 26, 2025. https://cllsociety.org/2025/02/rebranding-watch-and-wait/.

Tomer, Adie and Lara Fishbane. "Coronavirus Has Shown Us a World Without Traffic. Can We Sustain It?" Brookings Metro. May 1, 2020. https://www.brookings.edu/research/coronavirus-has-shown-us-a-world-without-traffic-can-we-sustain-it/.

Tonorezos, Emily, Theresa Devasia, Angela B. Mariotto et al. "Prevalence of Cancer Survivors in the United States." *Journal of the National Cancer Institute* 116, no. 11 (2024): 1784–1790. https://doi.org/10.1093/jnci/djae135.

Tsiouris, Angeliki, Nadine Ungar, Monika Sieverding, et al. "What Is the Image of the 'Typical Cancer Patient?' The View of Physicians." *American Journal of Men's Health* 15, no. 2 (2021): 1-11. https://journals.sagepub.com/doi/10.1177/1557988320988480.

Turner, Victor. *The Ritual Process: Structure and Anti-Structure*. Aldine, 1969.

Umberson, Debra and Jennifer Karas Montes. "Social Relationships and Health: A Flashpoint for Health Policy." *Journal of Health and Social Behavior* 51, suppl. (2010): S54–S66. doi: 10.1177/0022146510383501.

Vardi, Nathan. *For Blood and Money: Billionaires, Biotech, and the Quest for a Blockbuster Drug*. W.W. Norton, 2023.

Varul, Matthias Zick. "Talcott Parsons, the Sick Role and Chronic Illness." *Body & Society* 16, no. 2 (2010): 72–94. https://doi.org/10.1177/1357034X10364766.

Yanez, N. David, Noel S. Weiss, Jacques-André Romand, and Miriam M. Treggiari. "COVID-19 Mortality Risk for Older Men and Women." *BMC Public Health* 20, no. 1742 (2020). https://doi.org/10.1186/s12889-020-09826-8.

Yang, Shenmiao, Neil E. Kay, Min Shi, Curtis A. Hanson, and Robert Peter Gale. "Is Unmeasurable Residual Disease (uMRD) the *Best* Surrogate Endpoint for Clinical Trials, Regulatory Approvals and Therapy Decisions in Chronic Lymphocytic Leukemia (CLL)?" *Leukemia* 36 (2022): 2743–2747. https://doi.org/10.1038/s41375-022-01699-7.

Zuckerman, Phil. "Does Prayer Work? Yes and No." *Psychology Today*. September 30, 2019. https://www.psychologytoday.com/us/blog/the-secular-life/201909/does-prayer-work.

Index

About the Author

DAVID A. SNOW is a distinguished professor emeritus in sociology at the University of California, Irvine. Before joining UCI in 2001, he taught at Southern Methodist University (1975–76), the University of Texas, Austin (1976–1987), and the University of Arizona (1987–2001), where he was head of the Department of Sociology for almost a decade. He earned a BA from Ohio University, an MA in urban studies from the University of Akron, and his PhD in sociology from UCLA.

His teaching and research have concentrated on collective behavior and social movements; socioeconomic marginality with an emphasis on homelessness; social psychology with a focus on framing processes, conversion, and identity; religion and the persistence of belief; and ethnographic field methods. He is the author or co-author of numerous articles and chapters on these topics, and of twelve academic books, including the award-winning *Down on Their Luck: A Study of Homeless Street People* (with L. Anderson).

Dr. Snow is past president of the Society for the Study of Symbolic Interaction and the Pacific Sociological Association, and vice president of the American Sociological Association. He was a fellow at the Center for Advanced Study in the Behavioral Sciences at Stanford, and a recipient of numerous scholarly awards, including the American Sociological

Association's 2025 W. E. B. Du Bois Career of Distinguished Scholarship Award, the association's highest honor.

He is a veteran who was drafted into the US Army in the late 1960s and was employed afterward for a year as a juvenile parole officer in Cleveland prior to initiating his graduate studies. He was married for thirty-seven years to his late wife, Judy, who succumbed to a long battle with cancer, and has been with his current partner and wife, Roberta, for the past twenty years. He has three children and four grandchildren. In addition to relishing the time he spends with them, he enjoys reading widely, cooking (particularly French and Italian cuisine), lap swimming, walking, listening to music of all kinds, and traveling and hanging out with Roberta, family, and friends.